Prai

'[Corness] ... warrants high praise for sticking to the high road in "Farang". This enjoyable, 330-page ride on a three-wheeled cuttlefish cart dodges most of the potholes that cripple most foreigners books about Thailand. The ones that are unavoidable are negotiated with the even temper of an old hand.'

- Paul Dorsey, *Daily XPress*

'Like all good doctors and authors, Dr Iain Corness provides comfort for the aches and pains of ex-pat life. He chronicles the frustration and misunderstandings that go hand in hand with applying for a house loan, to getting married or buried, illustrating them in a series of delightful and insightful stories that will amuse, inform and stimulate anyone who has ever travelled to or settled down to live in Thailand. Finding the right balance between your own values and adapting to those in a foreign land is never easy, but the good doctor has written a prescription that is not hard to swallow: it requires a large dollop of humour mixed with a portion of patience, and a teaspoon of goodwill. Having read the stories, I am feeling better already.'

- Christopher G. Moore, author of the critically acclaimed and best-selling *Land of Sunshine* trilogy

'If anyone was equipped to write a series of short stories on life in Thailand from the perspective of the *farang*, it must surely be Dr Iain Corness. No detail of Thai life—big or small—escapes the good doctor's microscopic examination in his wickedly funny musings on ex-pat life. What makes his stories so compelling is his gentle understanding and good humour, recounting examples of the idiosyncrasies and frustrations faced and felt by many western visitors when they first come to Thailand. I could not stop laughing or nodding in agreement as I enjoyed his delightful and insightful stories.'

- Gary Stubbs, *Queensland Business Acumen* magazine

'This book highlights so many of the wonderful differences of living as an ex-pat. Dr Iain Corness, the *farang* in this book, takes you through these differences with a self deprecating humour, but you can see yourself in the same situations. A genuinely insightful look at our lives, portrayed in a very witty fashion.'

- Graham Macdonald, Vice-Chairman, British Chamber of Commerce, Thailand

'Ripper yarns with an Asian twist—focused wit and original wisdom from the Doc who has done most things, all successfully.'

- John Weinthal, Writer and Broadcaster, Kuala Lumpur

'Not only does Dr Iain see the things that make up Thailand, but he experiences them as well, bringing up unseen aspects and presenting them to the reader in a very humorous way.'

- Lang Reid, *Chiangmai Mail*

FARANG
THE SEQUEL

DR IAIN CORNESS

PUBLISHED BY MAVERICK HOUSE PUBLISHERS.

Maverick House Publishers, Office 19, Dunboyne Business Park, Dunboyne, Co. Meath, Ireland.

info@maverickhouse.com
http://www.maverickhouse.com

ISBN: 978-1-905379-63-7

5 4 3 2 1

The paper used in this book comes from wood pulp of managed forests. For every tree felled, at least one tree is planted, thereby renewing natural resources.

A CIP catalogue record for this book is available from the British Library.

Dedication

This book is dedicated to the three generations of women in my life.

My dear old Mum, 92 years old as I write this and has put up with me for 68 of them.

My lovely wife Som, who has already put up with me for eight years of her life, and hopefully will for another 30.

My wonderful daughter Marisa, who I hope will understand her father for many years yet, provided I release enough fish (the answer is inside this book)!

Acknowledgements

It is customary to thank all kinds of people who have helped in the writing and publishing of any book. I am no different, and I do believe I have a debt of gratitude to many people.

I must start with my publishers, Maverick House, especially Jean and John, who had faith in me. John did warn me that unless my name was JK Rowling or Dan Brown, I was never going to make a fortune as an author. I did suggest that I change my name to John Kenneth Rowling, but I was ignored. So be it. But I have to say it is fun to see your name on the front of a book!

There are also many people who had suggested topics for this new book and I do thank you.

Of course, there is my lovely Thai wife Som, who patiently explained much of the intricacies of Thai society and customs, but still wonders why they would be of interest to the western reader.

Finally, there were all those people who read the first book, who went out of their way to tell me that it had entertained and even inspired them. That, probably more than any other reason, inspired me to continue writing. I thank you all.

Iain Corness

Pattaya, Thailand, 2009.

Contents

Introduction

When I wrote the first 'Farang' book, I had no thoughts of writing another. Getting a book published was the same sort of thing as riding a bicycle. Once you had mastered the art of two wheeling riding and remaining upright, you didn't have to do it again. That was how I thought of being an author.

I have to say I was more than delighted by the reception received by that first book. Even when I had the first copy in my hands, it was still somewhat unbelievable.

The first week I saw the book as the number one bestseller, I couldn't believe it. I rushed out with a camera and took a photograph of the earth shattering occasion. Not just a book, but a bestseller as well.

When it went into the first reprint, I knew it had hit a popular nerve somewhere with the *farang* population, and I began to get questions as to when the next one was coming out, followed by the official request from my publisher, Maverick House, to begin writing again. I signed the contract in May 2008 and began writing, and so you now hold 'Farang the Sequel', thank you for buying it and I hope you like it.

Karaoke

In the first 'Farang' book I claimed that karaoke was Japan's revenge for WWII. Although it might seem controversial, I still adhere to that theory. Listening to karaoke is pure torture of the ears and nothing else could possibly come close to it.

Unfortunately for me, in Thailand it is so popular that it has become an almost compulsory social practice. At the end of any function, the karaoke machine is dragged out and some chap, several sheets to the wind, gets up on stage to thunderous applause and shrieks of encouragement to emulate Frank Sinatra with an out of tune version of 'My Way'.

However, it doesn't end there. More misguided souls will then rush to the stage and present the warbler with roses, followed by more enthusiastic shrieks from the audience, and so he begins to sing again. I have always been very against applauding, it only encourages them. This is definitely cringe material.

Karaoke and its compulsory nature in Thai society was really brought home the other day when it was announced that the hospital was going to put on a dinner for the doctors at a well-known hotel. The director of the hospital himself even gave me a personal invitation. How could I refuse? There was, however, one catch. After dinner there would be a karaoke session, and every doctor was expected to give a performance. A party piece. I hadn't been involved in anything like that since I was eight years old. Whether I liked it or not, I was expected to 'sing a song', as the Thais put it.

I began to think of the time I was last on stage to give any sort of performance. I was about 12 and played the part of a legless fighter pilot in the school play. My role consisted of sitting on a wheelchair and exclaiming, 'Kysh (which was, incidentally, a totally ridiculous name for a man-servant), answer the door.'

I was then shot and the chair and I were wheeled away stage left.

That part, however, didn't even include the daunting task of singing a song. I considered trying to weasel my way out of this impending croaky karaoke by explaining that I had been allowed to miss choir practice at school because I was tone deaf, and eventually they made my absence compulsory. After some thought I surmised that perhaps my complete lack of singing ability might not be as big a deal as I first feared. In fact, in Thailand it seemed to make me a prime candidate for karaoke performances. Ninety percent of Thai Frank Sinatra impersonators can't sing either.

Having accepted the inevitable that I would have to get up on stage and actually sing something, the next problem was finding a song that would possibly be suitable. My lack of experience as a singer means I do not have a bunch of songs in my head and I definitely can't just pick any one and begin to warble. No, I was going to have to be a little bit smarter than that.

I worked out that if I sang anything that anybody was likely to recognise, my total lack of talent would be excruciatingly obvious. The solution to this would be to sing something Australian, something which had never made top of the Thai pops. Kylie Minogue, Australia's singing budgie, was definitely not the way to go, but a little known Aussie ballad might just do the trick. It was then I remembered the song 'The Pub with No Beer.' This was a song performed by one of Australia's country and western stars, the late Slim Dusty and stemmed from a true story in WWII in which an outback pub really did run out of beer. In Australia, that would be tantamount to bringing down the government—if it hadn't been wartime.

Thanks to my friendly neighbourhood search engine, I got the lyrics, and thanks to my memory I could remember the tune. I practised all afternoon and then asked my wife Som if she would come listen to me. Clearing my throat, in the safety of our marital bedroom I began to sing.

Ballad and I passed our first hurdle with a less than enthusiastic response from my wife, but thankfully with no outright jeering. And so, with the words copied on to a sheet of paper, I went to the dinner. I had hoped that I would be called very late in the evening, when most people would be tipsy, but I was out of luck. I was down as the third act of the evening. I approached the stage and nervously began my solo performance. I very quickly decided two stanzas of chorus and another five in the middle was far too long, so I hope Slim Dusty would have forgiven me for cutting it down to five in total. The final line of the song, 'Than to stand in the bar of that pub with no beer,' rolled off my lips and I beat a hasty retreat stage left before there were too many calls for an encore.

The hospital CEO was waiting as I returned to my seat and congratulated me, saying, 'You see, that was easy. We're having another dinner at the end of the year and this time it's two songs, and one of them has to be from Isaan.'

It is August as I write this. If I practise every day, I might just be able to do it. However, I think I will borrow a concept from the Beijing Olympics Opening Ceremony and lip-sync it. It could well be an answer to all my karaoke problems.

An Admiral at the elevator

I was saluted by an admiral this morning. It wasn't just a perfunctory touch of the peaked cap, but a full-blown naval salute, complete with an exaggerated click of the heels. There he was standing outside the elevator, resplendent in a dazzling white uniform, complete with pinned-on campaign ribbons, three gold rings around the sleeves and his peaked hat positioned at a jaunty nautical angle. His boots were black patent leather with metal plates affixed to the inside of the heels that produced a loud clicking noise as the heels were brought smartly together. I should have been honoured.

However, my 'admiral' was no highly decorated naval man, but the elevator attendant at the hospital. He seemed very proud of his position and his uniform. In fact, there were similarly dressed attendants for all the elevators at the hospital, all equally uprightly naval in their bearing. My late father, who had been in the

Navy during WWII, used to say the Navy maxim went, 'If it moves, salute it. If it doesn't, paint it.'

My admiral and his friends are indicative of a certain phenomenon in Thai culture; this is the love of uniforms. Take a look at a photograph of the Thai parliamentarians on official duty. The entire 300 plus contingent are dressed in whites, complete with ceremonial sashes and campaign ribbons. It makes no difference that the closest any of them have come to action under fire has been crossing the road at lunchtime, especially since Thailand has not been to war with anybody since fighting the fallen French in WWII in Indo-China, over disputed territory in Laos and Cambodia (1940-1941). The win prompted the unveiling of the Victory Monument in Bangkok; however, the hard fought territories were apparently handed back to the French in 1946, after the French provisional government threatened to veto Thailand's membership in the United Nations. My 'Admirals of the Elevators' were certainly not around then.

There were other minor conflicts, the most recent significant one with Laos. Fighting broke out in December of 1987 in a dispute over land claimed by Laos, which considered the territory as part of the Laotian Botèn District in Xaignabouri and by Thailand as part of Chat Trakan District in Phitsanulok Province. That war ended about six weeks later on 19 February 1988.

I do not consider the highly publicised 'War on Drugs' waged by now deposed Prime Minister Thaksin

Shinawatra as a true 'war' as we know it. I am also choosing to ignore the (in my mind political) war in Iraq, where in 2004 Thailand provided the 10th largest contingent to the Iraq coalition, but were not frontline aggressors.

Mind you, I mentioned crossing the road at lunchtime for a reason. This is still a very hazardous undertaking. Even at the traffic lights, since all Thai drivers are congenitally colour blind. Traffic lights in Thailand are only advisory, not compulsory.

Step down in the hierarchy and all government officials (AKA public servants) will come to work in a military-style light khaki uniform, complete with epaulettes and more campaign ribbons.

Even the nurses and nurse aides in the hospital have very rigid dress code rules. This even includes photographs, sent through the internal mailing system, of how to arrange the scarf around the neck and how to keep their biro pens neatly in the pocket.

We have changed the security guard company at the hospital too. The new lot wear khaki, complete with Scotland Yard chequered caps, lanyards, boots, intercoms and whistles. Be found transgressing and you will be given a severe whistling. This need for uniforms is one of many sociological differences between Thais and westerners. Where individuality is considered a plus in the West, this is not true for Thailand; everyone must fit into a group, from family and upwards. This begins in schoolchildren, where they all wear uniforms from kindergarten onwards. Usually white shirts for the boys and blue or black shorts and similar for the girls, but with a pleated skirt that hangs below the knees. Within one day, Evan's white Kindergarten 1 shirt changed colour. Like a chameleon, he can adopt the hue of any background. I pity our washing machine at times.

By the time the Thai child reaches university, he or she is still in uniform, but as opposed to the secondary school outfits, the 'regulation' university outfit for girls is a short black skirt, complete with daring splits up the back. This tight skirt has a black belt, but there are no belt loops on the skirt, so the belt just sits there over the hips. The end of the belt is also held in place by a paper clip in the middle of the back. Perhaps this is to stop students leaning back and falling asleep.

The skirt is worn with the tightest shirt you could ever imagine, with the buttons straining in the buttonholes. Every university student wears one several sizes too small. I believe they think this makes them look as if they have large bosoms bursting for freedom. Interestingly, the silver buttons you see on the outside of the shirt are purely decorative. The closure buttons are hidden behind the silver ones. As an aside, the equally tight police uniform shirt has buttons down the front, but the closure is actually under them and is a full-length zip.

I found an interesting blog the other day started by a young university student called Alitta who wrote, 'I had to wear the uniform since I was in a kindergarten until I was a senior in the university. Asked if I loved wearing the uniform, my answer would be "absolute yes!" I have found no drawback of this kind of school rule so far.

'It was good that in the morning I did not have to be busy selecting clothing for school, I just prepared the uniform at night and that was so comfortable. Dressing in the school uniform creates a positive thinking towards people, dressing neatly is needed anyway.'

This is not a forum to debate the psychological needs of various races, but suffice to say Alitta's concept that wearing a uniform 'creates a positive thinking towards people' would not be one held by children from western countries.

In that light, my admiral fits in admirably. Perhaps I might salute back tomorrow morning, just to see what he does, though I vaguely remember being told that you don't salute if you are not wearing a cap. And I am not going to start wearing my father's old Navy hat for anybody.

The bicycles

When Little Miss Marisa was three and a half years old, she began pestering her mother and me for a bicycle. All the other children in our small village had bicycles, but as our daughter was younger than the others, I was reluctant to purchase her one. The fear of her falling off was foremost in that decision. Call me an over-protective parent if you like, I won't deny it.

One evening we were in our local Tesco-Lotus superstore, doing our obligatory grocery shopping, complete with Little Miss and two-year-old Little Mister Evan. We went in opposite directions and met up at the checkout.

'There are little bicycles on special,' said my wife. 'Only 590 baht (less than nine pounds sterling), and they have trainer wheels each side.'

Despite my misgivings we returned to the Friday night Tesco shopping frenzy and had a look at the special bicycles. Even a quick glance would confirm that these were no *Tour de France* racers, and would probably last three months if we were lucky, but at that price, could we complain?

'Are you sure she could ride one?' said I, as a last ditch effort.

'Yes, she is riding one at her school,' was the reply.

'Bisikun, bisikun!' said Little Miss as soon as she spotted them.

'Daddy wants to see if you can ride one,' I replied cautiously and a little negatively, but Little Miss needed no further discouragement. She hopped on and to my amazement pedalled away skillfully, through the legs of assorted shoppers, and disappeared from view.

After five minutes I began to get a little anxious, but since children are universally indulged in Thailand, even by busy shoppers, I should not have worried, as she reappeared from behind us, with a beaming smile that could have lit up a football pitch at night. That bicycle was definitely going to be hers. My wife then said, 'What about Evan? If Marisa gets one there will be fights over it. Should we get two?'

Feeling quite sure that he would not be able to manage it I put him on one of the bikes and looked to see if his little legs could manage a complete rotation of the pedals. Not quite, but not far off, and if I lowered the seat a little, it could be possible.

I agreed with my wife that we would get two and lifted young Evan off the bicycle, only to find that the bicycle came with the boy. With a vice-like grip on the handlebars, and his legs locked around the frame, there was no way this bicycle was going to escape from his clutches.

And so we approached the checkout, me dragging one bicycle with boy attached, while Little Miss pedalled regally behind. The checkout staff were very amused, and very helpful. They collected the price tags from the bicycles to scan them and after payment, our entourage made its way to the car park. Little Miss dismounted and her bicycle was put in the back of the wagon. I lifted Evan off again, and once more the entire outfit came off the ground, so he and bicycle attached, were placed in the rear of the car for the trip home.

Of course, the saga of the bicycles does not end there. By the next day we knew why they were so inexpensive. These were not just cheap Chinese bicycles, but I think were even cheaper copies of cheap Chinese bicycles, probably made in some native forest in Borneo or on some small Pacific island somewhere. Evan's front tyre was flat already. It was obviously time to go to the motorcycle repair shop up the road from our village. Bicycle and boy, carried by Dad, asked if we could get some air.

We were allowed some air, but that did not fix the problem. Removal of the tube from the front tyre showed it had more leaks than the American CIA. However, for only 70 baht, our friendly motorcycle repairer supplied a new tube, fitted and inflated and bicycle, boy and Dad were able to trundle home.

Unfortunately, this was no one-off failure, so we are now on first name terms with the village motorcycle man. His name is Somchai and I am 'Papa'. Since then we have had three new inner tubes between the two bicycles, and Little Miss's chain comes off regularly.

'Bisikun broken,' I was met with on several afternoons, along with a tearstained face. Fortunately she now knows that Dad can put it back on. On a good afternoon I am met with a 'Bisikun not broken' and a bright smile.

It became increasingly obvious that these bicycles were high maintenance items. It was back to Tesco-Lotus and several hundred baht later I was in possession of enough spanners and screwdrivers to get an aforementioned *Tour de France* racer running again, without resorting to banned substances for either bike or rider. Despite my misgivings, both bicycles were giving good service after six months. Evan enjoys crashing into his sister, but Marisa can now visit Insi, her five-year-old boyfriend with his own bicycle, six houses down, and together they pedal around the village, emanating that warm glow that only young love and a bicycle can produce.

The scenario reminded me of my own childhood, where it was quite safe to pedal around one's neighbourhood without adult supervision. Alas, that is no longer possible in the western world, but in Thailand, the children in the village still look after and play amongst themselves, and all the adults will care for any scraped knees and will drive slowly around, giving children the 'right of way'.

*Twelve months later: despite all my misgivings as to the quality of the bicycles, they are still both going. They need assorted nuts tightening every few weeks, we (or rather—they) have worn out two sets of trainer wheels, but fortunately my Tesco-Lotus sells them as a set. The inner tubes as supplied by the friendly chap around the corner are also bearing up well, and the tyres only need pumping up about once a month. The only other item of note is that Insi fell off his bicycle showing off in front of Little Miss and knocked out a front tooth. His father has banned him from riding, but I see that he sneaks away for a friendly ride around the block by using Evan's bicycle. Nothing, not even love, will get Little Miss to part with hers.

A nation of shopkeepers

I believe it was Napoleon who rather disparagingly called Britain 'that nation of shopkeepers'. Despite British surnames like Baker, Butcher and Smith which are derived from their forefathers' old trades, Thailand is much more deserving of this title.

In the first volume of 'Farang, Thailand through the eyes of an ex-pat' I mentioned one of my favourite shopkeepers, the 'Sticker Man', whose mobile shop almost defies description, but that was just one example. There are so many more examples, as everyone in Thailand seems to have a small shop selling something. For the purpose of this exercise, I am ignoring the armies of Avon and Amway ladies, who are always ready to pounce on unsuspecting guests at a dinner party.

I was reminded of all this last night when the family went to celebrate *Loy Krathong*, one of the most romantic Thai festivals dating back over 700 years.

Way back then, in the reign of King Phra Ruang, a famous Brahmin priest had a very beautiful young daughter called Nang Nopamas. She married this Buddhist king, but she followed the Brahmin tradition of her family in which one prepared suitable offerings for the spirit of the river. These were beautiful small 'boats' (*krathongs*) within which you floated your cares away.

Nang Nopamas was also the most beautiful woman, so today, even after 700 years, all the women dress up for the celebration.

My wife had decided it was time for us to be a little more traditional and let the children help in making our own *krathongs*, rather than purchasing one from the thousands offered from the pick-ups parked all the way along Jomtien Beach. After all, in these days of austerity, the 20 baht paid per *krathong* could be spent more productively elsewhere. For example, the local shop at the end of our street will sell me a can of beer for around that sort of money (definitely more attractive than a boat made of banana leaves).

There were so many pick-ups selling *krathongs*, it was almost impossible to park on Beach Road. In between the shop-houses are industrious families cutting up banana trunks to be used as the base for the floating arrangement, and folding the banana leaves into something resembling lotus blossoms. The family members make a production line, with the youngest and fittest sawing away at the trunks, the old grandmothers carry out the final decorations, and the end result is flogged by father from the family pick-up.

On the night of *Loy Krathong* there were many more entrepreneurs waiting to see if they could liberate my cash from my wallet. We had hardly sat down in the deck chairs (20 baht each) and reached for a beer (100 baht, now there's inflation for you) when the first of the old crones appeared thrusting a firework (100 baht) into Miss Marisa's eagerly waiting hand. Little Miss, then aged three and a half, is completely savvy with the 'possession is nine tenths of the law' concept and instinctively takes all items proffered (and some not proffered). Before 'possession' became absolute, the said firework was removed from her grasping hand and returned to the vendor, with the first of my chorus of '*Mai Ows*' (No thank yous).

Next up, at least a few milliseconds later, was the chap selling the *kom loys* (another 100 baht). These are mini hot air balloons made from polyethylene film and a paraffin candle as the hot air source. Fortunately the paraffin candle's life is finite, otherwise they would be finding the non-biodegradable balloons on the moon. No, they all eventually end up in the sea and even more eventually, are returned to the shore, for as long as we have a moon dictating the tides. Some *kom loys*, like the American space shuttle, are refurbished to fly again next year. Who said the Thais are not interested in the renewable eco-system?

We begged off the *kom loy* squadron (like the local taxi baht buses, there was one every 30 seconds) as the food sellers had spotted our table was not groaning with edibles. The first of these restaurants on the move are the traditional ones who carry both the product and the oven to cook it on. Steamers with prawns cooking away are placed beside you to tempt the palate. Ditto the calamari cooker. The squid got the nod (another 60 baht gone). However, modern commerce dictates 'instant' food-to-go, as per the American concept of family fodder, and the Thais have adopted and adapted to this new trend. Trays of deep-fried breaded prawns, green mango salad and similar items all in polystyrene boxes are paraded past you. The food may not last forever, but the boxes will.

Of course, what makes all this beach commerce even more exciting, is that it is actually against the law. To begin with, the sale of fireworks is illegal, as some western country has deemed them to be far too dangerous. The Health and Safety wallahs in the West will allow you to throw blancmange, as long as it is only semi-set, but nothing else that could be construed as, or used as, a weapon. So, all the fireworks for sale are black market items, and who could possibly resist the black market? And yes, I know there are inherent dangers, but that is what parents are for, to teach restraint and circumspect.

Even the food sellers, both traditional and 'fast food' are supposed to have a City Hall license to peddle their wares on the beach, but along with the license goes certain cash payments under the table so the vendor can be advised of the raids by the boys in brown (the police). It is a common sight to see vendors sprinting down Beach Road, being pursued by the vigilant authorities. Please note that I've written 'vigilant' not 'vigilante'. I am sure the authorities are aware of the difference.

That was just *Loy Krathong*, but there are many more SME's (Small to Medium Enterprises) you can find on any other day or night. Go to any of the racier streets in towns in Thailand and you will see someone walking down the street selling sexy underwear which is being modelled on a plastic torso being held aloft by the seller. This niche in the marketplace comes from the fact that the ladies of the night spend all day in bed recuperating, so cannot go shopping at the usual times, and the more successful ones will also spend most evenings and nights in bed, hence the need for 'home deliveries' of such working necessities as frilly knickers.

In fact, closer inspection of the night hawkers' wares will reveal everything from the aforesaid knickers, to blouses, skirts and even high heeled shoes. Naturally, food vendors are interspersed with the clothiers, with the full range of delicacies from *Som Tum* (papaya salad) through to the deep-fried beetles. Yes, if you are a nocturnal worker, the shops will come to you.

In our little village of 30 houses, we too could just sit there and wait for the shopkeepers to call. Little Miss Marisa knows every honk, whistle or tune that denotes the motorcycle and sidecar vendors such as the BBQ sausage man, the ice cream man and the *Som Tum* lady. Actually, it is great fun to watch all the village children perched on the top of the ice cream trike, whose vendor takes them all for a slow ride around the village. I am sure he blows the profit from his flavoured ices in petrol, but he and the children appear to enjoy the experience immensely, and so far, none of them have fallen off.

No, there are many kinds of shopkeepers willing to call to our home, welcome or otherwise. We would never starve, the windows will always have curtains and there will be a channel to watch on the TV while we nibble on BBQ items.

And finally, I read in the paper today that one of Thailand's banks will come to you to sign up your housing loan and presumably bring the money. The West may have drive-thru banks, but in Thailand they deliver to your door.

Thailand's cost of living

The question 'How much does it cost to live in Thailand?' is one that ex-pats are asked many times by people from overseas. After they have walked around the Thai markets and marvelled at shirts for 200 baht and shoes for 500 baht, and ate at the food stall for 100 baht they then imagine that the cost of living here must be peanuts compared to their western society.

I have to admit that I too fell into that trap of looking at my Australian salary and thinking that I would live like a king if I relocated. However, answering this question is almost as hard as answering the question, 'How long is a piece of string?' I can give you some idea of the costs involved in living in this foreign country though. But remember the cost of living is increasing, almost daily (petrol has doubled in 18 months), so this can only be a guide.

Before giving you a breakdown of how much it costs for Som and I and our two children to live, I must try to show you how we live, and at what standard. I honestly believe that to live successfully in another culture, you have to, as much as possible, maintain the living standards you experienced back home. It is very possible to live in Thailand for 100 baht a day and many Thais do. However, if you were an ex-pat here, would you be prepared to live on rice, rice and more rice, flavoured with a very wishy-washy fish stew? You will live in a wooden hut somewhere up-country, and your hobby and relaxation will be drinking a bottle of Chang beer at night. If you are lucky, some unsuspecting rich (by comparison) foreigner will be brought to the village by some bar girl ('Look what I managed to snaffle!'), and the evening's party will be paid for by him. Tomorrow's feast will be too, after the Bai Sri ceremony where white strings are tied around the couple's wrists, and the poor man thinks he has actually married the paragon of virtue he met at Sexy Legs a Go-Go last week.

Sorry to disappoint, but the only legally binding marriages are those registered at the local *amphur* office (see 'Farang, Thailand through the eyes of an ex-pat'). Bai Sri string falls apart on the third wash, as do many of the 'marriages' with the chrome pole palace ladies.

I am not prepared to live like that, even for 100 baht a day. I'm sorry. I've said before that if you ever find me sitting in a bar drinking warm beer at ten in the morning, dressed in a grubby singlet and colourful tie-dyed drawstring cotton trousers and a pair of those dreadful coloured plastic scuffs on my feet, then send me back where I came from. Unfortunately, there are ex-pats who do live like that. Many of them are known as the 'Balloon Chasers', this nickname comes from the fact that bars will celebrate birthdays by putting on free food, generally a pig on a spit, and let the passers-by know, by having brightly coloured balloons around the doorway. For me, that is not living, that is just an existence, and not why I came so willingly to live in Thailand. I'm not even that fond of the poor pork on a pole.

In Australia, where I lived for too many years, I would have been considered upper-middle class. I had a successful business, and by maximising tax deductions I was able to lease expensive motor cars, and so was able to make my fantasy of having a Porsche a reality. My Australian wife had the usual small Japanese runabout. I had a three-bedroom house with a pool, and the compulsory trip to the expensive pool shop every Saturday morning for more chlorine to stop the water going green. Anybody who has owned a pool will understand the pool experience. (I am convinced that the only pool worth having is one in the house next door!) My wardrobe was smart, without being sartorially splendid and my shirts were clean and ironed. We ate out at least three times a week and would go to the movies perhaps once a month.

I expect that I am thought of as a middle class ex-pat in Thailand. I do not have a Porsche, and in fact one will remain out of my reach for several lifetimes, even if I start saving now. Although daily transport for me is a 10-year-old Daihatsu Mira with 150,000 km on the clock, all 850 cc of asthmatic three cylinders, it is enough to carry me from home to hospital and return. (If this book sells well enough, I am looking at a Mazda 2 for 2010. Thanks for helping me move up.) My Thai wife has a larger Japanese runabout, as is needed with two small children. This carries assorted school books, school bags, school socks and shoes and containers that have been used for the nauseatingly smelly durian fruit beloved by my wife and children. I do not drive this vehicle until it has sat for several hours with the windows down. Better believe me, even Thai hotels will not allow guests to bring this fruit into the hotel. People have fled establishments thinking that somebody has died in room 24 A.

We have an almost new three bedroom house with two bathrooms, for which we thank the bank each morning and pay a mortgage to it every month. We do not have a pool, and neither does the chap next door, though the village development does have one. Perhaps this is even better than one in the house next door.

I go to work each morning, dressed in the same professional style I did in Australia, and eat lunch in the hospital coffee shop. As a family, we eat out at least once a week and go to the movies perhaps once a month.

You can see that I have attempted to maintain the same standards I had before although some of the expensive excesses are no longer within our reach. I really do miss that Porsche, though it would be totally impractical on Thailand's overcrowded rut-infested roads, with its kamikaze motorcycle riders that appear every three seconds. But if I do get left a million dollars by some long-lost uncle, I'll be round at the Porsche dealers the next day. Make that this afternoon.

So back to what it costs to live like this in Thailand. This is our monthly budget as of June 2008

	Baht	Euro
Mortgage	15,000	335
General living expenses	20,000	446
Health insurance	5,000	111
Phones	3,000	66
Electricity	3,000	66
Water (trucked in)	1,500	33
School fees	10,000	223
Maintenance	5,000	111
Fuel (two cars)	10,000	223
Car expenses	5,000	111
Restaurants, movies etc	5,000	111

The raw total is therefore 82,500 baht (1,184 Euro at today's exchange rate). Whilst this is much less than the cost of living in a western country, it should not be forgotten that wages here are also considerably less. That is, unless you are an ex-pat on a short-term contract, being paid at western salary levels.

So there you have it. To have a similar standard to what I had in Australia, it takes a figure approaching 100,000 baht a month if you are to save for items such as holidays, trips overseas to see relatives and the like. It is certainly not the 100 baht a day that I have often heard quoted.

Of course, there will be those who will question my figures and point out that if I lived in a country village, life would be much cheaper and possibly just as enjoyable. However, I work in the Bangkok Hospital Pattaya where I want to be, my children have easy access to good private schools (which are relatively very expensive, but the children can now speak Chinese which will stand me in good stead when China takes over the world next year), and I enjoy being part of the crazy society in Pattaya. I do recognise that I pay for these privileges, and so will you, if you wish to live at what I consider to be a good standard.

The singlet and cotton pants and plastic thongs is not an option for me. I am no way a snob, but I do have my own personal standards which I apply to myself. In Thailand we all have choices. I have made mine. But as I am not a 'cheap Charlie balloon chaser', it is not a cheap choice.

Toilets

There are many who have written about the Asian squat toilet, a device that invokes fear in most westerners. And so it should. Western and Asian toilets require anatomy at opposite ends of the scale.

Now, before someone leaps up and states that we are all the same, let me assure you that we are not. Medically there are many differences between *farangs* and Asians, Thais in particular. Let's start with the issue of hair. We all know that Thai women have wonderful long, straight, black hair, and while western hair has an even more wonderful colour range there is much more to it than this superficial difference.

Asian hair is circular in cross section, while the *farang* lock is oval. The circular cross section results in hair which is naturally straight, and does not tangle. However, the oval cross section makes for hair which is wavy, or curly, and naturally tangles with its neighbour.

Our skins hold another difference, and I don't just mean the colour. Whilst darker coloured skin offers more protection from the UV rays of the sun, and results in less skin cancers for Thai people compared to the white skinned foreigner, the Thai skin is also more prone to what is called 'keloid' scarring. This is the unsightly overgrowth of skin tissue following trauma to the skin. How many Thai ladies have you seen with thickened growths on the point of their shoulders? Lots. I'd guess that 99 percent acquired this condition after landing on their shoulders when falling from motorcycles.

This is an additional problem for the cosmetic surgeons. The medical tourist from the West has his or her face lift (yes, a lot more men are going under the knife these days) and is almost guaranteed a great result with little visible scarring. On the other hand, cosmetic operations on Thai women are much harder to hide because of the keloid tendency. Check the armpits of the next well-endowed Thai lady you meet and you will probably find small scars. These are keloid clues to the origins of the silicone valleys.

You might be wondering to yourself what all this has to do with squat toilets? Not much, but there is another difference which does. This is elasticity of connective tissues. A few years ago, the western world was suffering from an epidemic of a compensable condition called RSI, or Repetition Strain Injury. In this condition, the forearms would swell, it became painful to move the hand up or down, and eventually the person had to go off work. It would settle with treatment, but on returning to the same repetitive job, the condition would return. Some workers became totally incapacitated, and financial settlements ensued.

However, whilst RSI was bubbling away in the West, I was on one of my sojourns to Thailand, and met up with the Occupational Health Unit from one of the major teaching hospitals in Bangkok. On asking about RSI, I was met with blank looks. It wasn't a problem. To demonstrate this, they took me to a fish canning factory on the outskirts of Bangkok. This featured a long conveyor belt with women on each side, repetitively turning cans and product. This is the ideal situation to produce RSI but none of the women were suffering or had suffered from the condition.

Do you need further evidence? Try sitting down with your feet delicately out behind you, while holding your hands in the 'wai' pose in front, as every Thai person does when they visit the temple. You and I fall over sideways. In fact, the only way I can do this is to lean on a convenient temple pillar. You see, the Thai people are much more supple than the average westerner. For another demonstration of this fact, try squatting on your heels. Every Thai person can do this. And most *farangs* can not. We just fall over backwards, usually accompanied by screams of laughter from the Thais watching us.

These facts bring us to the squat toilet. Every Thai can squat, and place their feet flat on the foot prints either side of the low squat toilet and wait till Auerbach's plexus has done its thing, (that is the plexus of nerves involved in assisting defecation). Perfectly balanced, perfectly poised and perfectly natural (for a Thai). For you and I, gentle reader, this is a hazardous manoeuvre at best, and a total disaster at worst.

When confronted with an Asian squat toilet, the only way you and I can do it is to take off your trousers and underdaks, place your feet widely either side of the stunted pedestal and sit on the porcelain footprints upon which the Thai would normally (and naturally) stand.

Unfortunately, just the simple act of the bowel motion is not the end of the story, is it? We all want to wipe our bums, and Asian toilets do not have loo paper. In its place is a container of water and a dipper. Somehow (and I write 'somehow' because I don't really know how) you splash water at your fundamental orifice, and then pour more water into the bowl, using the dipper, until you have waved goodbye to last night's dinner.

By this stage, your shoes are wet, your backside is dripping and your handkerchief is needed, but not to wipe your nose. Dispose of the hanky later wherever you can.

So much for the squat toilet. However, in Asian houses and businesses where a western style toilet is installed, you will find two additional items. One is a bum-washing hose, a sort of serpentine French bidet idea, and the other is a small garbage pail. There may also be a sign in Thai, which you cannot read, but with a small pictogram indicating that loo paper is not to be put in the toilet. Hence the garbage pail.

Thai people seem to have this incredible fear that if the paper gets into the system, it will immediately block up. This is despite the fact that Thai toilet tissue is so thin it is almost transparent. This is one area where I feel the West is definitely light years ahead.

In any discourse on toilets in Thailand, one should not forget the unisex toilets, which abound in the bar areas. There may be two separate entrances, but inside it is definitely nonsegregated. There will be urinals of greater or lesser odour, usually with sections of cut limes (probably left over from some customer's whisky, lime and soda) or ice cubes (probably ditto) lurking in the bottom. I must say I enjoy seeing how many ice cubes I can melt with one bladderful, but that is only if I have the toilet to myself. Call it childhood repression or something, but I cannot pee if I am sharing the area with some little half-naked dolly bird in knee high boots eating *som tum* from a polystyrene container.

How many of you, especially those over 50, will admit to total failure to pee under these circumstances? Even when it may just be another chap standing at the next urinal? Rather than admit failure, I have seen me press the 'flush' button and then go through the shake and tuck routine. I am sure there must be a name for this condition, but have been too embarrassed to ask Dr. Jimmy, the friendly urologist at the hospital. It is my secret, which is now shared with the other 5,000 readers of this book. But any of you who have been to an Asian toilet, will know what I mean.

Finally, if you are ever at the Chatuchak weekend markets and find yourself caught short, do not go to the public toilets. The pedestals seem to have disappeared, leaving a yawning and vile smelling chasm in the ground. The results of falling or stumbling into it does not bear thinking about. Walk out to the street and pee in the gutter, but if you need more than this, walk under a Tuk-Tuk and get taken to hospital. It is infinitely safer than trying a Chatuchak hole in the ground.

Footnote: I had just written the above when the very next day I read in the *Bangkok Post* the following: 'Sewerage drains exploded in Chatuchak district yesterday morning, injuring a man and damaging several shophouses. The man said he heard a loud noise and saw flames coming out of the drains along the route. Staff from the Pollution Control Department said they found methane measured at 150 to 200 parts per million. This level of methane could easily ignite fires, especially if someone dropped a cigarette.'

So there you are. You have been warned, yet again.

Land of smiles, or land of contradictions?

'Always expect the unexpected' is one of those hackneyed phrases you come across a lot in life. In the case of Thailand, however, it couldn't be more applicable. This really is the Land of Contradictions. And sexuality, real or imagined, certainly comes into it.

A couple of years ago, while trying to promote Bangkok as the fashion capital of Asia, one of the catwalk models had a 'wardrobe malfunction' (thank you Janet Jackson and Justin Timberlake, you will always be remembered for your 'wardrobe malfunction' at the Superbowl half-time show, if nothing else). Anyone who has ever watched the Fashion TV show will be aware that titillation is the draw card (I love that word 'titillation', so apt when applied to the half-naked female breast).

The fact that a nipple popped out as the female clothes horse made her way down the catwalk should have really gone unnoticed—not in Thailand. There was outrage, which could be heard all over the country, fuelled by the Ministry of Public Decency. Actually, it was the Interior Ministry when I think about it, the section of the government that decreed we all had to be home in our beds by midnight, though they did later relent and allow tourist areas to stay open till 2 a.m. This led to the formation of a new branch of constabulary, who I call the Fun Police, but that's another story.

Let's get back to our fashion model. This wanton display of naked nipple was decried as being 'un-Thai' and besmirching the good name of Thai women. Since then, I believe fashion models have to wear brassieres. We'll have no more of that naughty stuff here.

Public morality and outrage surfaced again when an aspiring actress wore a very revealing outfit to a movie launch in provincial Thailand. She wasn't wearing any knickers. 'No undie Monday' had arrived in Thailand, or so it seemed. In the end, the offending garment was displayed to show it had built-in knickers. That was not enough for the baying hounds of public decency; she was cut out of the film and publicly reprimanded by her university.

Just in case you think that moral outrage has taken over Thailand's image after dark, rather than one of Go-Go bars and horizontal folk dancing, let me introduce you to an advertisement from one of the supplements belonging to the *Bangkok Post*, the largest circulation English language daily in this country. This newspaper, incidentally, was morally and righteously offended by the nipple and knickers incidents. In fact, they gave them a lot of column inches, but no photos. *Bangkok Post* is definitely not the *News of the World*.

The supplement in question was called *Guru* and this one was dated 26 September 2008. Please turn to page 33 if you have hoarded your *Guru*'s; you will see a full-page advertisement for 'Superba 100' vowing that it will 'Increase blood circulation and penis strength, prolong erection and prolong post-ejaculation erection.' The distributor even offers a Money Back 'Quarantee', which one presumes is a Thai 'guarantee'. How you would prove your claim is not given, but it doesn't end there.

On the lower half of the advert, the same people sell 'Max Estroginie' which promises to 'Arouse him with big boobs and tight puss'. The mind boggles (I'm not sure what my cat has to do with all this). This wondrous cream will, according to the advert, 'Increase and firm your breast' (do you have to buy a second tube for the other one, I wonder?) and will give the perspiring arouser 'refreshing pink nipples'. In a land of dusky maidens with dark brown nipples, this must be some powerful medicine. Perhaps it is neat bleach? In the adverts defence, it does state in parentheses that it takes ten days.

Finally, there is the 'Verginal Intimate Serum' which promises it will 'Give back a youth virginity to your vagina and illuminate surrounded the skin' (exact quote and spelling). This, I presume, must be some sort of flashlight to illuminate the area. Batteries not included, I would imagine.

I wonder if the British tabloids would print this advert, even for swinging Londoners? While Page 3 girls with pneumatic knockers are an integral part of the British newspaper culture, is it ready to illuminate vaginas yet? Somehow I doubt it. But here in straight-laced Thailand, in the number one newspaper defending public morality, we have such advertisements. Everywhere you turn, contradictions abound.

On the other side of the public decency coin, we have the government trying to legislate that during the water throwing festival (read manic water fight) called *Songkran*, young women should not wear skimpy tops held up by spaghetti straps. I suppose the lawmakers are worried that the girls might inadvertently expose their 'refreshing pink nipples'. Heaven forbid.

It gets even more basic than that. Anyone who has ever been here for longer than three minutes will have noticed that if a Thai girl bends forwards, such as over a desk to pick up a paper, she will automatically bring up her left hand to the neck of her dress, so that it does not fall outwards and expose her bra.

On one hand we have a country where women swim fully clothed, hold their necklines to stop exposing flesh, and must be seen to be modestly dressed, and yet on the other hand we have countless bars, chrome pole palaces, karaoke outlets, soapy massages and 'service girls'. These establishments offer dalliances for the man who has been gobbling down four capsules of Superba

100 at a time and could knock down walls with his willy, freely advertised in the nation's number one daily.

Undoubtedly Thailand is the Land of Contradictions, but would I want to change it? Not really. The contradictions themselves are all part of the unfathomable nature of living here, a country where you really can 'expect the unexpected'.

Hear today—
gone tomorrow

Hear today—gone tomorrow! For me, these days, it is more 'hair today—gone tomorrow.' All jokes aside, deafness is an increasing problem in Thailand, a fact which is being acknowledged by the various noise abatement bodies in this country (and yes, amazingly there are some).

Of course, the picture in everyone's mind when you mention Thailand is serenity; saffron robed monks walking single file, muted Buddhist chanting, smiling people giving each other respectful *wai's*, almost a silent Garden of Eden here in Southeast Asia. Unfortunately it isn't.

For some reason, noise seems to have become part of the local 'culture'. For example, when my wife wants to attract the attention of the lady across the street, she doesn't walk outside or call out from her gate. No, she just stands in our doorway and bellows. (These mild and demure Thai ladies have very large voices.)

How many times have you heard people screaming into their telephones? At volumes so loud they really don't need the phone at all. Go into shopping centres and be physically assaulted by noise levels so great they approach the threshold of pain. I personally experienced one promotion for children that had passers-by holding their hands over their ears, whilst two screaming and amplified MCs exhorted the children to crowd around the stage (and its boom boxes). The noise levels were simply horrendous. The resulting damage to the hearing of young ears could also be horrendous. Even walking down the street, your ears are assaulted, not only by motorcycles, but also by slow moving promotional vehicles with mobile boom boxes telling you all about the newest shopping centre. Where you can shop in comfort?

These promotional vehicles almost merit a story of their own. They travel in threes, one behind the other, and they have pleated material around the sides of the pick-up tray, like you see on official tables. They all have large loudspeakers mounted on them, playing a promotional message. This recorded message is played at full volume, but the three loudspeakers are not synchronised. You end up with noise that sounds as if it has been put through a food blender and then amplified to become even more distorted.

While on the highways and byways there is the constant blaring of motor horns of the buses looking for fares. Ditto the taxis. As you cross the street the beep-beep does not herald a warning, it is an invitation to flag the driver down.

With regards to all this noise, what does not seem to be understood by the public at large is that hearing, like eyesight, deteriorates over time. However, when damage is done to the hearing early in life and when the hearing loss that occurs through aging is added to this, you are guaranteed of increasing deafness as you get older.

My hospital has even just opened a hearing clinic, as the incidence of deafness is reaching epidemic proportions. (If it gets worse, the World Health Organization will be calling it a pandemic.)

Having been involved in industrial hearing protection in Australia for many years, we had to convince a reluctant workforce that it was necessary to wear hearing protection if the industrial noise level exceeded 90 decibels (dB) for a 40 hour week. In auditory terms this is known as a 'noise dose' of 1.0.

If the noise level experienced by the unprotected ear was over 120 dB, then the 'safe' exposure was measured in minutes. An example of 120 dB is the level reached by an ambulance siren—or a rock concert. I don't think we've quantified a Bangkok bus, but it would be up around 110 dB at least. Other examples are the hammer drill that you use to drill holes in concrete which operates at 114 dB or a headset for personal listening at full volume, so the 'safe' level here is 15 minutes a day.

Noise induced deafness characteristically affects the hearing at 4 kHz first, that is towards the upper musical ranges, and it goes on from there. If this noise induced hearing loss begins early in life, then the chances of the person ending up clinically deaf by the time he or she is 50 years old is very high, especially if the person is Thai.

So what can be done? Various research papers from around the world have managed to quantify the risk, and others have shown that although the risk is recognised by older children and young adults, they are not likely to do much about it. In some ways I can agree with them. Why bother going to a rock concert if you have to sit quietly to hear the music?

We know the problem exists. We know the relative 'safe' levels of noise exposure, but is wearing ear protection the answer? Quite frankly, this is a classic example of an ambulance at the bottom of the cliff when there should be a fence at the top. Preventive action needs to be carried out at the noise source. But that will be very difficult as the noise source is the Thai society at large. The Gardens of Eden are far from serene. In this situation at least, Thailand does seem to be far behind the western society. The 'Nanny State' has managed to protect the hearing of the population, but I cannot see universal use of hearing protection happening in Thailand in the foreseeable future, because always remember that Thailand means the 'land of the free'.

Perhaps now is the time for us *farangs* to start shouting at the regulatory authorities. And until they answer our call, remember to keep your children away from noisy shopping centre promotions, while they can still hear your instructions.

Diets

It is often said by those who should know better, 'You are what you eat.' This is, of course, total nonsense. Do vegetarians turn into carrots? Does a weekend BBQ turn you into a ground pawing steer, or in Thailand, a sick buffalo? Obviously not. You are a living, breathing human being. End of story. It is true, however, that the shape you present to the outside world does depend upon what you eat.

There is probably more rubbish written about diets and dieting than any other subject in the world. Every third person you meet is either on a diet, just got off a diet or is about to go on a diet (after the New Year, her son's Bar Mitzvah or the swearing in of the next US president.) There are countless numbers of different diets, from the Israeli Army diet where you eat nothing but bananas and sand, to others created by multi-level marketers where you make up and drink three sachets of expensive powdered goop every day that promises to get the weight off you in one week. It might take slightly longer, but as long as you keep buying the sachets, that's the most important thing.

The most important fact to remember is that dieting has nothing to do with big people, it is all about big business. Even if you don't buy the weight reducing sachets, you will be buying the diet books and scanning the supermarket shelves for 'diet' foods that turn out to be a little more expensive than the others. It's hard to see how this is the case when they aren't adding anything to the food, they are actually leaving sugar and other expensive nasties out.

Obesity was once a scourge exclusive to the western world, but it has now become another gift we have given to Asia, along with fast food and certain communicable diseases. Twenty years ago, Thai people were all small, the ladies had two fried eggs on their chest and that was it. Things have changed, and it can't be denied that Thai people are getting larger, in all respects. There is even a school of thought in the Thai-Chinese community that obesity displays just how much money you have seeing as you are able to (over) eat so well. The chrome pole dancers are needing stronger poles as the western food has filled them out to a stage beyond being pleasantly plump. This, of course, doesn't include the large silicon valleys women can instantly achieve with a trip to my hospital's Beauty Centre. And don't fall into the trap that breast enhancement is just for well-heeled tourists, many Thai ladies (professional and otherwise) line up for a new superstructure. Localised fat removal by liposuction is also very popular in Thailand, where slimness is revered. It doesn't include, either, the ladies from Isaan who still eat *Som Tum*. This delicious dish comprises scorpions, steamed water beetles, first cousins of the cockroach, and sticky rice. This dish helps them to keep obesity at bay, and is impossibly spicy for any *farang* to eat. And anyway, the scorpion will make you vomit.

So where does the fat come from? My favourite obese lady was a patient of mine, who weighed 22 stone (150 kg give or take a little) and lived in Gibraltar. We had to use two scales to weigh her, standing there with one foot on each. When I suggested she could perhaps be eating a little too much she replied, '*Me no como nada por dos annos.*' (I have eaten nothing for two years.) If she was telling the truth, I shudder to think what she weighed before.

I hear a lot of talk from fat people about their 'bad metabolism' and how lucky thin people are to have a 'good metabolism'. Other than in a few spectacularly rare endocrine diseases, 'bad metabolism' is not to blame for the shapes of 99.999 percent of fat people. I apologise if I am crushing any myths here.

Metabolism is, however, involved in the fat cycle. By this statement I am referencing the mammalian metabolism which is the same for all of us. You, me, the lady next door and even the local *soi* dogs in your street (of which you will never see a fat one). Understand the following equation and you have now become your own personal dietician: 'Input exactly equals output, plus or minus what goes into store'.

It means that the energy source (food and drink) equals the energy output (physical and mental effort), plus or minus what is stored (or removed) from your body as fat. This equation is independent of whatever you call the energy, be that kilojoules or calories or sugar lumps.

In simple terms, if the input and output are the same —then your weight stays the same, as zero goes into or comes out of the storage fat. If the input is greater than the output, you have an excess and that goes into store and you put on weight. If the input is less than the output, then you are in a deficit, the body makes up the energy levels it needs by burning up fat from the store, so you lose weight. Honestly, it is that simple.

So here we go, if you really want to lose weight (and you must do or you would have already skipped this page and gone onto the next), I present the well tried, proven and effective diet that I have modestly called the Dr. Corness 75 percent diet. (Atkins did it for his diet, why shouldn't I do it for mine?) This diet is guaranteed, which is more than I can say for the others. It will get the weight off, and keep it off and you do not have to count one calorie or kilojoule or sugar lump. If by following this diet you have not lost weight after four weeks, write to me and I will write back and tell you that you are a liar. That is my guarantee.

This simple diet works by decreasing your input by 25 percent. In other words you can have 75 percent of what you would normally eat and drink every day. If you have four cream buns a day, you can have three. If you eat a kilo of beef every night, you can have three quarters of a kilo. That's right, you don't need to deny yourself anything. However, you do need to be honest with yourself. Count those slices of bread at lunchtime. Is it six or is it really four?

I suggest to my patients that they write down everything they eat for a week, work out the 75 percent of this and then stick to it. If you think your dinner looks lonely on the plate, put it on a three quarter sized plate, so it fills it. And enjoy your cream buns while you lose weight.

This diet works because by decreasing the input by 25 percent, you will be in the situation where the input is less than the output, so the body needs to drag the deficit out of the store, which is the fat that is deposited under the skin and around all your organs.

Of course, if you want to really ensure there is a deficit, you can always increase the output at the same time. A daily walk that you didn't do before, or even a walk around your office block at lunchtime all helps. Walking to someone's office in your building, rather than lifting the telephone, also uses up energy. Use the stairs, rather than the elevators.

The only downside to this diet is that you will not see instant results, and you will feel hungry for a few days. The reason for this is that the storage fat has to chemically change into 'energy' fat before it can make up the deficit, and this takes a few days. Your body will not automatically do this either, until you are in the deficit situation. After a week you don't notice it, and after a fortnight you will see the weight loss happening.

By the way, I do not recommend changing to an Isaan diet. Your metabolism is not ready for such a dramatic change. Trust me—I'm a doctor!

The 'real' heroes

The original 'real' hero was the first man to eat a raw oyster. His name has not been recorded. The next real hero was a Frenchman called Garnerin who jumped out of a hot air balloon in 1797, strapped to a parachute of his own design. Just imagine his nagging doubts as he stepped out of his wicker basket. This was the first successful parachute jump.

Note that I said successful. A couple of years before, an Englishman had thrown his dog out of a similar gondola. No records have been kept of the first canine landing on earth, but no news is probably not good news. My personal theory is that Rover probably made a nose-dive and gave birth to that strange species of dogdom called 'The British Bulldog'.

I cannot claim to be a real hero, as nothing I have ever done could be claimed to be a world 'first' though in retrospect, riding a speedway motorcycle for the first time aged 42 isn't bad, I suppose.

However, Monsieur Garnerin and I do have something in common. Both of us have parachute jumped. He went on to do it many times, but I will probably just rest on my laurels. After all, having now done 'it' there is not much more to be achieved by doing it again. Once more on reflection, if I had just thought this way after that first sexual encounter, life would have been a lot easier in its post pubertal progression, but then, think of the fun I would have missed.

But I digress. I have lived all my life with a mental check-list. 'Things I have to do before I die,' is the rough working title. That list has included riding the aforementioned speedway motorcycle, riding 'in the chair' of a racing motorcycle side-car outfit, scuba diving, motor racing in all classes up to Formula 5000 and flying in every aviation device since Icarus, from helicopters, gliders, Tiger Moths, ultralights, microlights, flying boats and even a blimp, but the last one was the parachute jump.

Twice I had the opportunity of scoring it from the list, but each time there had been last minute snags, usually in the form of a newspaper report that another parachute jumper had gone the way of the Englishman's dog. In fact, over 30 jumpers land terminally awkwardly each year in the US. But the list was not to be denied.

While driving along Jomtien Beach Road one day I received a telephone call which began, 'Would you like to do a parachute jump?' I had to answer in the affirmative and it just went on from there. What was on offer was a tandem jump with free-fall from 10,000 feet.

On the surface it sounded interesting. At least one had someone to blame on the way down if anything did go wrong. 'You left the parachute—where? Thanks very much!' On the spur of the moment, the die was cast. Like Luke Reinhardt in 'The Dice Man' (a wonderful thought provoking book) once the decision was made, it had to be acted upon. The date was set for the following weekend. I was, however, given a guarantee that we would come back to the ground. However, the speed of arrival was not covered by the same lifetime warranty.

Parachute jumping is actually very popular in Thailand, with the climate being stable, and the military very happy to be involved. Several world records for intentionally falling out of aeroplanes have been set in Thailand, the latest being when 400 people jumped from five Royal Thai Air Force C-130s over Udon Thani, Thailand in 2006. Wearing red, white and blue jump suits, the skydivers, who hailed from 31 countries, had about 80 seconds to form a flower-like arrangement in the sky. At over 23,000 feet, it was dubbed one of the most difficult mass sky dives ever. And before you ask, I was not one of the 400.

But back to the tyro in Pattaya. There had been no time to back out, or even read up on the subject, so there I was on the fateful Saturday afternoon, in the air and heading to the jump altitude. It was not a graceful start to the event, on my hands and knees shuffling backwards towards the space where a door used to be on the plane before they started hacking it up for the parachutists conference. On my back was Khun Vinai, my 'buddy', the man who was clipped to my harness and who was going to get me safely to the ground from our cruising altitude of 10,000 feet.

We inched out the door, the wind clawing at my legs as they emerged into the slipstream—and then it happened. I fell like a stone down a bloody well, the horizon blurring as I tried to focus and work out what was happening. My first thoughts were, 'Oh sh*t! I've left him behind! And he's got the bloody parachute!' Then equally as sudden, we changed from vertical to prone, I got the pre-arranged three raps on the shoulder to tell me he was still there and to spread my arms out and we were skydiving.

The noise, as you hurtle towards the earth at 120 mph, is almost deafening, but then into focus came the other three skydivers who had been in the plane with me, one with a helmet TV camera, one shooting stills, and the third was Patrick, the Belgian paratrooper, giving me the thumbs up of encouragement.

The free-fall was 5,500 feet taking approximately 35 seconds, with the chute being deployed at 4,500 feet. This was like an invisible hand suddenly and roughly yanking you into a vertical position again. I groaned as the crutch straps of the harness bit into my dangly bits, but then everything changed again. An eerie quietness enveloped us after the roar of the free-fall, as we floated gently towards *terra firma*.

Khun Vinai gave me the controls for the parachute and showed me how to turn one way and then another. The chute itself gave little flapping noises, somewhat akin to the flap of the sails in a yacht, but much softer. It was so peaceful and relaxing, I began to wish we could have stayed up for longer, but gravity will not be denied, as the Englishman's dog would have testified. Khun Vinai took the controls again and we slowly glided towards the drop zone, landing softly, back on solid ground. Well, relatively softly, despite my inadvertent summersault complete with co-pilot.

I sat there, still shackled to my buddy, as people came up to congratulate the novice after his first jump. My grin ran from ear to ear. A lifetime's ambition had been achieved. The last one on my list.

There had been a quiet professionalism displayed by the skydivers which was very reassuring for the tyro. Even on the 20 minute plane trip as we climbed to 10,000 feet (great views, by the way), they were solicitous of me and my welfare, and at the end shared my elation, as if it were their first jump too. But that was far from the truth—Khun Vinai having completed thousands of solo jumps and I was his 194th tandem.

If you wish to try something that the vast majority of your friends have not got the 'bottle' to do, then think about a tandem jump. You do not need to be super-fit, and as I mentioned before, they will guarantee to get you back down to *terra firma*. The experience is something that will last a lifetime. Believe me—no matter how short.

Postscript: The plane I had travelled in crashed on take-off one week later. No casualties, but a sobering thought that none of us, including Monsieur Garnerin, the Englishman's dog and myself, should take air travel lightly.

A night out with the boys

There are plenty of husbands who have regular nights out with the boys. I am not really one of them, as quite honestly I prefer the company of my wife on a night out. Perhaps, I have just reached the age where I've seen it all before, although I refuse to admit to any of it.

However, in 2008 I had great experience that really did come under the heading of a night out with the boys. I spent several hours backstage at the Tiffany's Transvestite Cabaret Show for *Pattaya Mail TV*, and by the time I left I had a better understanding of local show biz, plus an unabashed admiration for both the performers and the workers behind the scenes.

It should also be remembered, that whilst getting up close and personal with transvestites is something most unlikely to happen to you in the West, transvestites or ladyboys (*katoeys*) are totally accepted in Thai society and culture. Do not forget that Thailand is one of the few countries in the world to have three official sex classifications—men, women and women of the second category (*katoeys*).

Holding my hand (metaphorically, I might add) was the Technical/Creative Director Ken Smith, an Australian show biz professional, who gave me an insight into the running, planning and perfecting that goes into a production like the Tiffany's Show. Having had a little experience of the theatrical business and the people who work within it, I was all prepared for the fact that the Tiffany's 'girls' would have nightly spats, the boys likewise and that there would even be some across the great divide. 'Bitchy' is the best word to describe what I expected. When Ken said that wasn't the case, I frankly accused him of being somewhat economical with the truth. However, he was correct. We set up our TV crew backstage in the changing area, which was basically a unisex dressing room, and watched them all go quietly and efficiently about their business. There were no arguments, no petty jealousies and no drama to be seen.

With Pattaya Mail TV being a family show, I instructed the cameraman that whilst the performers were quite happy for him to be there, I did not wish for any footage of the prominent 'silicone valleys' which were everywhere. With 85 percent of the performers being ladyboys, there was a fair percentage of silicone bouncing around. There was a complete week's production from Dow Corning on titillating display (couldn't let that pun get away).

The next amazing fact I discovered backstage was the show lacked a timetable. There was no board stating that the Chinese number would commence at 7.45 p.m., and the following French number should be ready to go on at 7.56 p.m.

'It just happens without any fuss,' said Ken. I didn't believe him, but once again, he was right. There were no rushed last minute preparations, no performers rushing around looking for their eye-shadow or green lipstick, just a well-organised group slipping in and out of costume and waiting in the wings to go on and perform.

Being a performer is not all champagne and roses though. The Indian costumes which have two sets of additional arms and are worn on the back weigh a considerable amount. I did try one on for size. 'You'd have to be a man to carry one,' said Ken whimsically.

The backstage crew who get the sets ready is another well drilled group, dismantling one set and readying the second very efficiently. There's even a group to park the 'elephant' used in the Thai number, for example.

If you have visited Tiffany's Show recently, you will have seen the act where one of the girls floats through the ether, suspended on wires, and is lowered to the stage from about eight metres in the air. Before she went on I saw her quietly praying, and wondered why. I was invited to follow her up to the launching pad eight metres above the stage and I could immediately see why. It was a long way down, and undoubtedly she was hoping providence would keep the wire intact. In fact, it was so scary climbing up the ladders to the top platform that my chief cameraman refused to do it. Fortunately his junior was not afraid of heights, and filmed the take-off, while number one cameraman recorded the landing.

After observing the Tiffany's Show *katoeys* at close range backstage I was taken with the professionalism they showed. They are a different group of people in our society, but ones that display an amazing talent, given the correct vehicle to put those talents on show.

On TV I facetiously said that there were two toilets backstage. One clearly marked 'Boys' and the other clearly marked 'Boys!' I made that up. The only sign that would be necessary would be 'Toilet.' They are a completely integrated group.

One of my friends who has seen the spectacular cabaret shows in Las Vegas has also been to Tiffany's Show and says that the Pattaya show is better than the famed American ones. Having never been to Las Vegas, I cannot comment, but I would say that my friend is not one who is prone to exaggeration.

Like so many features in Thailand, because it is always there, you begin to forget about it. This is a shame, as Tiffany's Show, despite having been around for about 30 years, has grown with the resort city, and is something that we can all be proud of. The general manager of the cabaret is Alisa Phantusak, who firmly believes that the transvestite cabaret is much more than just a tourist attraction; it is a genuine outlet for people of Thailand's third gender to be accepted and hold down worthwhile jobs. I am inclined to agree with her.

If you haven't been to Tiffany's Show recently, it is well worth the admission price and a 'must' for tourists. My thanks to Alisa Phantusak and Ken Smith for making it possible for me to have a rather memorable night out —with the boys!

Alzheimer's, and why
I don't have to worry

Alzheimer's is a particularly distressful disease. Not only for the sufferer who, in the initial stages can see their own mental faculties deteriorating, but also for the family around the sufferer who watch as the person they once knew and loved slowly disappears. The exterior shell is still there, but the inner person has long gone.

When I surprised everyone by reaching the ripe old age of 60, I had a couple of items on my mind. The first was where to hold the biggest birthday bash ever, and second was to look for signs of Alzheimer's.

The first was easy. With the help of my good friend Peter Malhotra, the MD of Pattaya Mail Publishing, my 60th birthday was celebrated around the pool of the Residence Gardens, a lovely serviced apartment development run by long term ex-pat Ib Ottesen and his lovely Thai wife Kannikar, with food from their Captain's Corner restaurant next door. Over 100 people turned up and some of the year's best hangovers were recorded the next day, including mine.

The second was not to be so easy. Facetiously, I have always said the acid test for Alzheimer's is as follows: if you can remember that you have forgotten something, then you haven't got it—but if you've forgotten that you've forgotten, then you do!

As you get on, there are all those wonderful lapses which we (older folk) call 'Senior moments'. Last night my old friend Alan (a year older than me) and I spent hours trying to remember the name of a film actor in the Great Escape—the one with claustrophobia who dug the tunnel. Now I know what you're thinking, but it wasn't Steve McQueen, he was the one who jumped the fence. It was Charles Bronson. Feeling better now?

Our joint brainstorming had failed to produce the name, so we decided to consult possibly the best guru ever invented for all those people experiencing the aforesaid 'senior moments'. This is, of course, google.com. With Mr. Google by your side, you can find (remember) almost anything. Even, in this case, the tunnel digger from the Great Escape. If that has jogged some memory cells, the others were James Coburn, James Garner, Steve McQueen and Richard Attenborough.

There are, however, certain situations that even Mr. Google cannot help you with, and the following is one of them. I am not particularly good in the mornings. I never have been, and will choose and lay out my clothes the night before, as my 'select clothes' mental switch does not turn on before 9 a.m. It is not advisable to ask me to carry out a physical task more technically difficult than cleaning my teeth before 8 a.m.

In preparation for my early morning ineptitudes, I leave my car in the same place each night, in the car port of the unoccupied house opposite mine. This worked well. The car was out of the rain and would not be hit by errant motorists coming up the street several sheets to the wind. This has a tendency to happen quite often in Thailand as breathalysers are practically unheard of and a 500 baht note pressed into the correct hands smooths over almost all such altercations. The 500 baht note is colloquially known as the 'purple persuader'.

One morning, with my clothes on, my medication taken and my children kissed, I walked out to the street to get into my car. I opened the other house's gate and there was no car in the driveway. In a moment of awful realisation, I thought someone must have stolen my car. However, this had to be impossible. Nobody would steal my car, why would they bother? In Thailand I drive the world's most banged up car; a Daihatsu Mira.

For those unaware of the Daihatsu Mira, let me paint you a picture of mine. My Daihatsu Mira is a small Japanese box that, on a three cylinder engine, delivers enough horsepower to get me to work and back at 80 km per hour on the flat. I usually find it best to keep away from hills. It is ten years old and has been lovingly ignored for at least eight of them. It is only washed when the rain decides to fall and oil is only put in the engine when the red light won't go out. It has a lot more contours in its panels than the manufacturers ever intended; these are the result of many altercations with various motorcycles. One of the worst was caused by an incident in which a Volvo attempted an illegal rear entry when I was stopped at some traffic lights. I remain heterosexual.

You can imagine, then, my surprise on this morning, when I discovered my car was missing. I had always been under the impression that I could leave it, parked at the side of the road with the keys in the ignition and nobody would take it. I would even be optimistic if I left it for a couple of months in a slum area. Yet, now, from outside my home it had disappeared.

It was then, as my head began to clear, that I heard Little Miss Marisa calling out to her mother.

'Daddy's forgotten where he left his car.'

I turned round and there she was, standing on our top step. Imperiously she raised her arm and pointed up the street.

'It's over here,' she said, pointing again with the finger.

And indeed, there it was, on our side of the street next to our garden wall. As my brain cells cleared, my memory returned. The previous night it had been raining, so I parked it as close to our house as I could and ran in, rather than running up from the usual parking spot and risk getting soaked.

Now, I have my second line of defence against Alzheimer's. My saviour is Little Miss Marisa, who, at four years of age, knows everything. When I cannot find my comb, wallet, pen or trousers, Little Miss knows exactly where they are. In fact, she has begun to make sure I am properly dressed in the mornings, with belt and tie and reading glasses in the shirt pocket.

As I typed this, I began to see another advantage in being a Second Time Dad. You are at the age where you need a personal assistant, and, luckily, you have recently grown your own.

The answer then, for those of you who are wondering if Alzheimer's will strike you down, is google.com and a four-year-old daughter. Having both, I do not fear for the future. And in case I have left you wondering, Colin 'the Forger' Blythe was played by Donald Pleasence in the Great Escape, and Marisa assures me that my collection of DVDs is in the spare room on the third bookshelf.

Being an atheist in a
Buddhist country

When you marry a Thai lady, you marry her family. I have dealt with this elsewhere in this book, but what is not so well known is that when you marry a Thai you become very personally exposed to Buddhism.

The official figures state that Thailand is 94% Buddhist, I have no doubts that this is correct (though I certainly regard some other 'official' figures as being open to question). Everyone from the motorcycle taxi rider on the street corner to the doctors in the hospital wear Buddhist icons of some type, either openly displayed or tucked into a shirt pocket.

It would be difficult to ignore the fact that we are living in a Buddhist country. There are *'wats'* (temples) everywhere and one source of information claimed there are 31,200 of them throughout Thailand. Nothing would surprise me. My wife, a devout Buddhist, goes to three of them regularly. Only another 31,197 to go.

Early in the morning, on my way to work, I will usually see the saffron robed monks doing their alms rounds. A householder will be crouched in front of them offering food, which is placed in the large alms bowl. This keeps the monk from going hungry and gives merit for the donor, almost like a deposit in a celestial merit bank.

One area where there is much confusion in the minds of the *farangs*, visitors in particular, is with the spirit houses, most businesses and residences have at least one pair. They see the Thai people reverently clasping their hands together and bowing to the spirit houses, and think that this is an act of Buddhist piety. It isn't. This worship is even older and belongs to animism. However, the Thai people seem to be able to integrate the two without one being done at the expense of the other. It is almost like being a Catholic and a Jew at the same time. There are certain inherent differences that would seem to make it impossible at first glance.

Even without being married to a Thai, Buddhism will impinge upon the *farang* whether they like it or not. There are many religious holidays during the year and some very auspicious 'Buddha days'. On these very important days such as Visakha Bucha, the bars must close, restaurants cannot serve alcohol and the convenience stores cannot sell alcoholic beverages. This, of course, brings howls of outrage from the resident ex-pats who expect to be able to consume alcohol on any day of the week that has a 'y' in it. Letters are written to the newspapers claiming that all holidaymakers who suddenly find they are arriving on a dry day will never come back, the experience being too excruciating to be repeated and the entire tourism industry will collapse. This is, of course, codswallop. Mind you, I have to admit that on these dry days I suddenly seem to develop a thirst that would drain a reservoir. Fortunately the old lady who keeps the shop on my street corner isn't fazed by any of this and a cold bottle or two can be purchased at normal price.

On the three main annual Buddhist festivals (Makha Bucha, Visakha Bucha and Asalaha Bucha) that celebrate events in the life of the Buddha, people go to the temples early in the evening for the Wien Tien candle-lit ceremony. After chanting, a sermon and some meditation, they walk mindfully three times clockwise around the temple buildings holding lotus buds, a lit candle and burning three incense sticks, followed by the faithful. The air is filled with burning incense and smoke from the candles as the congregation complete this most sacred of Buddhist celebrations in silence. They then place the candles and incense sticks nearby as an offering.

Obviously this is a very important time for Som, and rather than leave the children at home with me, we make it a family outing. I have to say I am very proud when I see the children showing due reverence. Whilst I chose an atheist way of life, at this stage the children are nominally Buddhist and I have no objection at all. On our last trip to the temple for Visakha Bucha I left Som to make her own devotions during the Wien Tien, whilst I took the children to walk with me. All three of us had bunches of candle, incense and lotus but Evan's candle, in particular, kept blowing out and a two-year-old voice would loudly exclaim 'Candle broken!' The gentleman behind us would offer a lighter and we would continue. It was a long three laps, but we made it.

At the end, one of the temple ladies (they are not all nuns) said that one of the monks was a *farang*, and asked if I would like to meet him. This particular chap turned out to be an Australian and he asked me if I were a Buddhist. When I said I was an atheist he replied, 'That's good, you're half-way towards becoming a Buddhist.' Phra Mark, as he is known, has become quite a good friend and although we do not go on pub crawls together we enjoy the odd afternoon chats sitting on the verandah of his '*kuti*' (very small house) in the grounds of the temple's meditation centre. He makes no attempt to indoctrinate me and neither do I with him. We have discussed reincarnation, which is one of the cornerstones of Buddhism, but is one of the first hurdles at which I tumble. (I have the same problem with the Catholic transubstantiation.)

Buddhism also plays a central part in our home. We had been together for about two years when Som asked if we could have the Buddhist channel on our TV. I said yes and was told that it was not available on our cable network, but we could get it via satellite. I did express some concern at how much this would cost as the commercial satellite providers were certainly not cheap, but the figure quoted was extremely inexpensive. The following week we were visited by a technician from Bangkok with a monk in tow, and the satellite dish, receiver and cabling were installed. We now had access to the DMC Buddhist network.

When you consider that Buddhism predates Christianity by 500 years or so, I thought it rather fantastic that this ancient religion was so up to the minute. The items on the DMC channel are very varied, including sermons done by a wonderfully laughing monk in Bangkok, cartoons for the children and even daily news broadcasts. The channel is also trilingual (Thai, English and Chinese), but we leave ours on Thai. I am not going to be seduced by a television screen.

In common with all Thai households and again most businesses, we also have a small shrine which has Buddha statues and various Buddhist amulets on it. My wife will do her daily devotions in front of this and will meditate kneeling before it. Som did ask me to try to meditate (so did Phra Mark) but rather than finding it a fulfilling experience I spoil the serenity of it all by falling asleep and snoring.

Donations to Buddhist charities and projects are also part of living with a Thai person. There are always envelopes being passed around for you to place a donation in, anything will do, whatever you feel comfortable with. Since Som believes that the money that comes into our household is from the sweat of my labour (seen in the fingernails chipped from typing), she always asks for my permission to make a donation. I find this rather touching especially after the western 'what's yours is mine and what's mine is mine' approach. I am told to say *'anumotana satu'* which apparently means that the merit will be shared. I just hope mine goes to a good home.

Just as western societies have adopted the Ten Commandments as a reasonable way of keeping society headed in the right direction, the Buddhists have theirs, called the Ten Precepts.

These are:

- Not to kill.
- Not to steal.
- Not to engage in improper sexual activity.
- Not to indulge in wrong speech.
- Not to take intoxicating drinks and drugs.
- To abstain from taking food at unreasonable times.
- To refrain from sensual pleasures such as dancing, singing and self-adornment.
- To refrain from using high and luxurious seats in order to practice humility.
- To refrain from wearing scent or garlands.
- To refrain from handling gold or silver so as not to incite greed.

As you can see, most of us would fail in that list somewhere (as do most Buddhists, I might add), but again they are reasonable rules for an orderly society. Incidentally, a monk has to be bound by 227 precepts, so the laity gets it easy.

At the start of this chapter I mentioned the wearing of Buddhist icons, and I also wear a very small medallion pinned in my shirt pocket. This was given to me by Som after we (I) had donated money towards some roofing for a temple in Bangkok. This was my token of '*anumotana satu*' and a thank you from the temple. I do not believe it changes my atheism, but I wear it as my 'thank you' to my wife and what she has done for me.

The price of Thai virginity

Many foreigners have the preconception that Thailand is a very free-wheeling and easy-going country. Go to the right areas of Thailand and a girlfriend for the evening will probably cost you about 1,000 baht. For misguided opportunistic swains, this means that all women in Thailand must be free and easy, and 1,000 baht will buy you everything in the love for sale stakes. Take that concept even further and there can be no value placed on virginity here.

It is in this misconception that many come undone. In my previous book, I described the plight of an inebriated young buck walking through the red light area of Pattaya who presumed that all females who were there were on offer. They are not, which he found out to his chagrin, when an attempted drunken fondle ended up in the girl screaming and his arrest. It was also the cause of the police assisting him to empty his wallet and donating the contents to the offended young lady to allow her to regain her honour. This was after a suitable small sum had been kept aside for the policeman's time and aggravation in dealing with this tipsy foreigner.

Another drama was enacted in my wife's village due to another one of these misconceptions. A (previously) virgin 13-year-old girl was found 'in flagrante delicto' with the 18-year-old son of a European married to a Thai lady in the precinct. The girl was living with her uncle, as her father was working overseas.

A meeting was immediately set up between the girl's uncle and the boy's father. Underage intercourse is against the law in Thailand and the boy would be looking at a jail sentence and a heavy fine. However, before the local police were notified of the crime, there was the chance of a negotiation for a 'get out of jail free card' (have you ever stopped to wonder just how much Monopoly has influenced our lives)?

It's worth noting that when I say 'negotiation' I really mean the act of money changing hands. In Thailand, everything has a price, even if it is not actually for sale. In exchange for the loss of virginity, the price of one million baht was put forward to stop the boy from being prosecuted. After all, said the uncle, there was not only the loss of virginity, the girl's social status in the village and her future dowry; there was the loss of face for him. The girl was in his care, and this situation was a bad reflection on him as well.

The ball was firmly back in the boy's father's court and another meeting was scheduled for the next day. In the meantime the girl was banished to her bedroom.

The immediate situation of the boy was not recorded, but he was not seen loitering around the village store. At this next meeting, the boy's father played his trump card to the million baht demand. He said he didn't give a toss what happened to his son. He was not going to pay anything. Send him to jail, he didn't care!

The uncle did not give in that easily. Thais are past masters of the art of barter for anything from hair shampoo to houses, and have been trading with Europeans for the past 500 years. The uncle began applying some subtle pressure. Perhaps one million baht was a little over the top, but if the police were brought in, the father would still have many financial expenses in just getting the case to trial. The discussions regarding the futures of the two young people were now down to what was important: financial negotiations.

These negotiations continued for a few days until the final sum of 300,000 baht was agreed upon. This would be enough to send the girl to a school in India, so her face would be saved (and her history forgotten). The boy could return to school and be saved from a Thai jail.

The preconception of Thailand's cheap and easy sex is most definitely refuted by this event. Even if paying 1,000 baht per night, that defloration behind the woodshed had cost father and son the equivalent of 300 nights of commercial sex. Even randy 18-year-olds might not manage that in one year. Mind you, there are not too many virgins in the red light district, despite claims you can hear any night at the local bar beer. 'Me virgin. Only work bar one week.' Translated from Bar Beer English to standard English, this means 'I used to be a virgin. I've worked these bars for at least a year.'

By the way, in case you wondered how a bar that sells beer is a 'bar beer' and not a 'beer bar', it is simple transliteration. In the Thai language, the adjective follows the noun, so you don't get a big bottle, you get a *kuat yai* which is a 'bottle big'. A bar with beer is then a 'bar beer'. Simple!

Of course, in the villages, if a resolution cannot be made between the aggrieved and aggrieving parties, then the local policeman is brought into the picture. His job is to dispense 'justice', summary or otherwise, using the Thai criminal code as a rough guide.

An example of this occurred when my wife visited her village. In such a small community, the whereabouts of everyone is common village knowledge, and so it was known that she was now living in Pattaya and married to a *farang*. The local village troublemaker saw her going to the temple and called out that she would need to make a lot of merit, because she was a Pattaya prostitute. 'Turn the other cheek' belongs to Christianity, not Buddhism, and my very offended wife immediately reported the lad to the police. You do not sully the reputation of an upright Thai woman and get away with it. Thailand may appear free and easy, but it isn't.

In no time at all, the young buck was summonsed to the police station and told he had to pay a financial compensation to my wife, plus an apology. Rather than doing that, he ran away to Bangkok where it would be very difficult to trace him. Did it all end there? Oh no. His parents were summonsed to the police station and told that if they did not get the lad back in three days, they would have to pay.

He reappeared and a suitable sum was handed over, which the policeman divided between himself and my wife. Justice was seen to be done. The guilty party suffered. The policeman was paid for being the prosecutor, judge and jury and my wife was mollified. Her slice of the fine she donated to the temple. Making merit would be much more valuable than the cash.

There are certain standards to be upheld in this country, and you can be sure that there is a monetary value placed on everything.

The Tuk-Tuk and the flamethrower

While I was writing this piece, George W. and his merry men were still raining fire down on Baghdad, which is probably why this tale came to mind. Many years ago, in my previous existence in Australia, I was the owner of a Thai restaurant called Thai Tasty, in Brisbane the capital of Queensland.

Thai Tasty was memorable for many reasons; it was the first 'Thai fast food to go' in Brisbane, it was my first foray into the food business, and it had a Tuk-Tuk. I have written about this elsewhere in this book, but this was a genuine Bangkok Tuk-Tuk I had imported via Sydney, registered it there and then brought up to Brisbane on a truck. I can still remember unloading it, firing it up and roaring off down the road. At the very first corner I thought I was going to topple off the vehicle. I quickly came to the conclusion it was a diabolical device and I began to understand why being a Tuk-Tuk driver is one of those occupations reserved for Thai nationals. It is! Most Thais have an ingrained talent that enables them to dodge in and out of chaotic traffic on the most unreliable of vehicles and come out at the end of their journey unscathed.

However, I persevered and the Tuk-Tuk soon became the symbol for Thai Tasty. I was to be seen all around the city on it and I soon became the target of my local Inspector Plod. He wanted to know why it was registered in Sydney, and I was in Brisbane. I could talk my way out of that one by saying we were in the process of changing addresses. He also decreed that it was a car so I had to wear a seat belt. My pleas that this strange vehicle was neither a car nor a motorcycle fell on deaf ears. Inspector Plod recognised two categories of vehicle only, and the Tuk-Tuk was not in his rule book. Since the thought of attaching a seat belt mount to the vinyl roof was more than faintly ridiculous, the Tuk-Tuk became parked at the front of the restaurant and only used for surreptitious nocturnal blasts around the block, taking the last few diners for the ride of their lives. By this stage, I must add, I had mastered the art of two wheeled cornering which resulted in predictable screams from the rear seat.

With the Tuk-Tuk no longer mobile, I devised another method of attracting attention to the restaurant. Hearkening back to Bangkok, where pavement kitchens are the norm, I would set up a BBQ satay stand on the footpath outside the restaurant. The sight and smell would quickly bring people to the grill, and one free satay would be enough to have them flocking in the door to buy more. Barnum and Bailey had nothing on me for promotional ideas.

I want you to now picture the set-up. As I was not lithe and limber like the Bangkok Thai ladies, I would set the charcoal grills up on two large boxes, rather than squat on the footpath. The best boxes were the ones that the take-away plastic bowls and lids came in and were about one metre tall. The way the Thais get these burners going is to heat the charcoal on gas wok cookers until the charcoal is red hot and slowly burning, then the hot coals are transferred to the BBQ. My method was different and quicker and involved the petrochemical industry. I would drizzle a large amount of methylated spirits all over the charcoal, throw a lit match on them and stand back. Within a couple of minutes the coals were cherry red and away you go; simple.

One Saturday I had set up the two BBQ's, sloshed the spirits onto the coals, torched them and went out the back to chat to the chef. Five minutes later I returned. BBQ one was a cheery cherry red, but BBQ two had not taken. Muttering, I picked up the plastic bottle of spirits, and began to really slosh the fluid over the coals.

The next second there was an almighty WHOOMPH and the plastic bottle in my hand swelled up, growing to twice its diameter and spat ignited spirits in a huge arc of flame from the neck of the container. Looking back, I really should have realised that some of the coals actually had taken and all that was needed was a bottle of methylated spirits for instant ignition.

Naturally, after a quick expletive, which referred to procreation, I dropped the bottle, just as a customer went into the restaurant, passing under the flaming arc. He ran up to the cashier, shouting, 'Fire! Fire!'

Flora, my Asian cashier, was not quite as quick on the lingo as she was on the cash register, and so turned to look at the menu board, softly repeating, 'Fire, fire,' mentally going through the English alphabet, while looking for the 'F' item which must surely come after Choo Chee Goong but before Gaeng Garee Gai.

In desperation the customer began yelling, 'Water! Water!' and this was something Flora did understand. 'Jug in bottom of fridge,' she said smiling, turning back to the cash register.

In the meantime, I had found that I was standing in a sea of burning methylated spirits, which had also ignited the cardboard boxes with instantly flammable plastic bowls and lids. Hopping up and down, while trying to stamp on bowls flambé, I was suddenly doused by a guy with two jugs of iced water. At that stage I didn't know what was worse—the hot-foot or the frozen *songkran* festival.

Needless to say, Inspector Plod was also summoned by the chemist shop next door, whose owner was convinced I was attempting to torch her building. This was followed by a call from my landlord advising that I was in breach of my lease as BBQ cooking was not allowed on the footpath.

Ah yes, the plight of the restaurateur is much greater than you would ever imagine. So next time you buy a satay from the lady on the street corner, just think of the tribulations she would have if she tried to set up in your home country.

Thailand—the world's kitchen

It seems like every year the Thai government comes up with another fanciful idea to elevate the kingdom, bring in more tourists, and generally give everyone a warm fuzzy feeling. Some of these are more successful than others, but at least they get an 'E' for Effort. This approach is better than sitting around moaning and groaning about the local economic problems, which unfortunately many of my *farang* brothers are wont to do.

One of these promotions was 'Thailand—the World's Kitchen' in which Thai restaurants overseas were encouraged to push Thai food and ingredients to help the local economy. There were good reasons behind this. Agriculture is the principal occupation of over half of the population, and half of these are rice farmers. Despite all the industrial development, Thailand is still an agrarian economy, living on the sweat of the Isaan farmers. The North-East of Thailand does do something else, other than export young ladies to the tourist spots—really. But if you don't read the business pages in the papers, you may have missed it in amongst all the anguish columns which feature young ladies from Isaan and heavily out of pocket love-sick young men.

In Thailand, rice, as a cereal, is the staff of life and the source of tradition and belief. It has played an important role in Thai society, providing a strong foundation for the evolution of all aspects of society and culture, as reported by the government's Public Relations Office. Rice is regarded as a sacred plant with a spirit, a life, and a soul of its own, just like that of human beings. To the Thai people, rice is guarded by the goddess Phosop, and rice itself is considered a 'mother' keeping guard over the nation's young and watching over their growth into adulthood. Heaven help those children who leave rice on their plates. My children are force-fed until the last grain has been stuffed into a less than appreciative mouth. Fortunately, being *farang*, I escape this ritual.

It is claimed that Thailand is one of the world's oldest rice-based civilizations. The evidence of a good quantity of rice in pottery fragments beneath a grave unearthed at Non Noktha village, Nong Na Kham sub district, in Khon Kaen province attests to the fact that rice had long been cultivated in this part of the world— for no less than 5,400 years. In the North, at Pung Hung Cave, Mae Hong Son province, rice husks were found in pottery, similarly dating back no less than 5,000 years. Goddess Phosop has done a sterling job!

The principal strain of rice is the *Hom Mali*, or Jasmine rice, and the Department of Agriculture's records show that this species of rice was first found in Bang Khla district, Chachoengsao province.

Thailand's reputation as the world's kitchen does not end with its rice. Other cash crops that make up the agricultural economy include sugar cane, maize, cassava, and an immense variety of fruits. The kinds of vegetables and fruits sent to the European Union and six other countries (Singapore, Hong Kong, Japan, China, Malaysia, and the United States) include green okra, ginger (tender and mature), baby corn, chilli (including dried chillies and cayenne pepper), asparagus, longan, durian, lychee, mangosteen, mango, tamarind (sweet, sour, and young), and pomelo. Japan also imports much from Thailand including 21 different kinds of vegetables.

Another thing to look at is how Thai cuisine has swept the world. In Australia in 1988 at the Expo held in Brisbane, Thai food was given a great deal of publicity and it was afterwards that I decided to open my own Thai restaurant. My establishment was the sixth Thai restaurant in a city with a population of one million. Six years later, when I sold my restaurant, there were 66 Thai restaurants in Brisbane; a ten-fold increase in six years.

The way I became a Thai restaurateur was rather fortuitous. My medical practice was doing well, but I was being hit badly by tax. Since I firmly believed in the popular bumper bar sticker of the day which stated that

'Taxation is theft,' I began to look around to see how I could diversify into some sort of cash business. Fast food seemed to be the answer, but I baulked at opening up yet another hamburger or fried chicken outlet. Mr. McDonald and Colonel Sanders were already well entrenched into the Australian society (as it is in Thai society these days).

You have to understand that by 1988 I was a frequent traveller to Thailand and had made friends and contacts in the kingdom. One of these was professional photographer Tom Chuawiwat, one of the chosen photographers whose work was featured in 'Thailand, Seven Days in the Kingdom' which was published in 1987.

I used to stay in Tom's fourth floor walk-up on Sukhumvit Soi 24 when I would come over on holidays. It was no real surprise when in 1988 he knocked on my door in Australia. He asked me if he could stay for a while. When I asked him for how long and he replied two years, there was only a second's hesitation before I invited him in to stay.

It turned out that Tom had decided to leave Thailand and wanted to settle in Australia. To become eligible for a resident visa he had to stay in Australia for two years and (in theory) had to fend for himself, so for him, I was the natural host. After a few days, I asked Tom what he intended to do for the two years, and he floored me when he said that he was a very good cook and thought he could distribute home-cooked meals as a way to support himself.

Here I was looking for a different fast food business, and providence had just dropped a Thai cook in my lap. The concept of 'fast' Thai food was born. Tom would cook a dish, and I would look at how to make it 'instantly' available. At first, freeze-drying and subsequent microwaving looked a possibility, but it didn't work. Still investigating just how to do it, I went to the best marketers of fast food—McDonalds, and studied just how they did it. Sitting at the back of a McDonald's restaurant I had one of those 'Eureka' moments. Big Macs were not made to order, they were already making Big Macs and just supplied one when required. What was even more clever (or obvious) was the fact that the rate of production was also responsive to the rate of demand. Not only was there no waiting, there was no waste.

I then looked at how we could do this in our restaurant and the application of the McDonald's principle was easy. We decided on using a bain-marie that would be filled with eight servings. The customers would be served from this and when the level got down to two servings, the cook would then make another eight. It was a simple idea, but effective. This was how Thai Tasty Takeaway was born, the first Thai fast food outlet in Brisbane. It was an outrageous success, and on busy nights would deliver almost 300 servings. We expanded and took over the shop next door to make Thai Tasty Eat-In, and we did deliveries using the aforementioned imported Tuk-Tuk.

In this way I did my bit to help Thailand become the world's kitchen, using only genuine Thai spices and ingredients in our dishes. All the other Thai restaurants in Brisbane said that our *Tom Kha Gai* was the best, and so in return for buying this book, I will give you our recipe at the back of the book. This was actually not one of Tom's but came from Sopa, our maid. It is much creamier than you will find here in Thailand, but it is absolutely delightful. To really appreciate this dish, take it as a soup, rather than eating it the Thai way of ladling it over rice. Enjoy!

Buying a new car— Thai style

Think back to the last new car you bought in your home country. You went to the showroom, expressed interest and were probably immediately roped in by an enthusiastic salesman who suggested you go for a test run. In many countries, you can even take the car home overnight, so that you can show it to your wife. Start to show some positive leanings towards this new car and the deals will knock you over, as the salesman attempts to get your signature on the bottom line.

It is very different in Thailand. I was in the market for a new car. My venerable, my old Daihatsu Mira was on its last legs. The patient had been resuscitated so many times, it was almost inconceivable that it could survive another major operation. No, I knew that my Daihatsu should be laid to rest with dignity. It had served me well for the 150,000 kms on the clock. It was time for a new one.

I went to the Bangkok International Motor Show, like all good motoring journalists, and whilst getting an overview of the cars on offer, saw a couple that sparked my interest. I approached one and all that happened was a young lady, who could not speak any English, gave me a brochure. Unfortunately, the brochure, which was in Thai, did not have a price on it, and having exhausted my (limited I grant you) Thai, I gave up at that point. The car was obviously not meant to be mine.

The other car company did have brochures in English (Hallelujah!) and a price, and as an extra bonus, the name of the sales person. I rang when I got back to Pattaya, or I should say, I got my wife to ring when I got back to Pattaya. Working on the principle that a Thai speaking to a Thai would produce a better outcome than a *farang* having a go at it, I waited for the result of the call. 'He has not got any cars left. He is very busy. He will ring us later.'

It was April when my wife rang. When I wrote this, it was August. I have given up hanging around near the phone. Either he is very, very busy or the manufacturer stopped production when they heard I was interested. Perhaps they were afraid I might not like it. It was back to looking for a new car locally. I went looking for a replacement at the weekend. What day of the week does a salaried employee have off so that he can go round car dealerships and look at cars? Sunday, correct. What day of the week do most of the dealerships close? Sunday, that is also correct. There seems to be something lacking here regarding the business acumen of the Thai sales force. Perhaps if the dealership was to stay open on Sundays and close on Mondays, it might get a better response? As with the lottery, you've got to be in it to win it.

Back to me and my currently fruitless attempts at buying a new car. Still on the lookout for something that appealed to me, I saw a very attractive car on the forecourt of a major dealership close to my home. There were many advantages to buying from this particular establishment. I could easily drop the car off for service, and the model I liked, white with two broad blue stripes over the roof and with big fat wheels, looked fabulous.

There was only one problem, the model on display on the forecourt turned out to be a private car. It was not a production car. It did not even belong to the dealership. I asked how much it would cost for another car, done exactly the same, all in white with two broad blue stripes over the roof, and with big fat wheels. They did not know. I wasn't going to give up that easily so I asked if I could go for a run in one of their demonstration cars.

'Yes, but not the same size engine.'

When I replied that it would be quite helpful if I could drive a car with the same engine as the one I was actually going to buy I was informed that wasn't going to be possible.

'Sorry, that one not going.'

Another salesman appeared. The reason the 1.8 litre car was immobile on the showroom floor was only down to a flat battery. Another car was driven into the showroom, the jumper leads were applied, and the demonstration model taken out into the sunshine for me to drive. Can you imagine what I was thinking as I drove down the road? 'I hope it doesn't stall on me. This car has a flat battery and nobody cared.'

Did this little scenario make me impressed with the dealership (or the manufacturer)? Lesson number one in the car salesman's manual—always have any car spotless, tuned, cleaned, with fuel in the tank and air in the tyres. In fact, when I did my brief 'apprenticeship' in a car sales yard as a university student, my job was to start every car in the morning and warm them up, so that they would then start immediately when any punter showed interest. I also had to get the dust off all the cars to make them look attractive. This lesson seems to have been forgotten in Thailand. In fact, I doubt if this lesson is even in 'Thai Salesmanship 101'.

The next warning bells about the dealership rang when I heard about some complaints from some dissatisfied customers. What I learned from these sources was that when a customer puts in an order for a car and requests particular specifications their car is not available for three months. However, if the customer agrees to a little 'under the table' payment the salesperson will be able to find the car at another dealership and have it brought down for the customer almost immediately. I have also heard there have been problems with test drives. Either they are refused outright or they consist of the salesperson putting the customer in the passenger seat and driving once around the block.

Considering that a new motor car is the second most expensive purchase in most people's lifetime, surely the Thai sales personnel could try just a little harder? It might even increase sales, and the profitability of the company, and we all know just how precarious that profitability can be in these troubled financial times.

No, it is very different buying a car in Thailand compared to buying one in the West. But in some ways, the uncertainty of it all makes it more exciting, I suppose.

Being yourself

One of the most endearing characteristics of Thailand is that the Kingdom offers you the opportunity to just be yourself. No matter how that 'self' is interpreted. If you want to be different, it is 'up to you', a phrase you will hear many times in Thailand. This roughly means that it is down to the individual, and nobody else, to take responsibility for themselves.

About once a week, in the late afternoon, a cyclist goes past my office. What catches my eye about him is the fact that he is always wearing a formal, tailed dinner jacket. He does not wear the usual formal black kind, rather one made of gold sequined material. He also has a hat made of the same material, with two large pink ostrich feathers on top. His trousers are equally studded with sequins, as are his boots. Flying from the back of his bicycle is a Union Jack, so one has to presume he is British. He is not advertising anything. He is (presumably) just being himself.

If he were pedalling down any UK high street, he would have people pointing fingers at his incredible outfit, and he would probably be physically assaulted by the time he got to the bottom of the street. Anyone 'different' is treated with mistrust. This is not the case in Thailand. Whoever, or whatever he is, he is not harming anyone. His decision to dress like that and pedal around is 'up to him' and I applaud his decision.

I experienced a little of this myself, without having to resort to sequins and ostrich feathers. Kim Fletcher from the (now) Jameson's Pub was putting on a 70's night, and everyone was arranging 70's costumes. The local tailors were inundated with *farangs* wanting Paisley pattern shirts and impossibly flared trousers. It became obvious that this was going to be some turn-out. Even Elvis and Evel Kneivel were coming. In fact, several of them would be in attendance. People were planning ahead.

I have to admit I had not, and on the morning of the 70's night I had obviously left it too late for the local tailors to knock something up. A suit in 24 hours perhaps, but a stage costume in six hours was asking a little too much. It was then I had a brainwave. The Malibu Cabaret!

Now, for those readers who have never been to the Malibu Cabaret, you are missing out on a great night. It is a cabaret like no other. The performers are a mixed group—boys, girls, ladyboys and even female impersonators. Admission is free and the price of food and drink is pretty reasonable. There are 80 performances every evening, and one of the best Tina Turner shows you will see this side of Las Vegas. It was lucky for me that I knew the chap in charge—Tina himself (aka Dwee). I explained my predicament and he told me to come round that afternoon and he would find something suitable. 'Something suitable' turned out to be a flowing pink dress with a bushy wig, a Shirley Bassey outfit, Dwee told me. On me, however, it was more of a Burly Chassis outfit, as I couldn't get the zip at the back to do up properly. As they say, beggars can't be choosers, so I took myself and my new pink ensemble quickly home.

Som burst out laughing when she saw it and said I really needed make-up to go with it. I thought of the old adage, 'In for a penny, in for a pound', and sat patiently while all the necessary items of make-up were applied. I now know I am pleased to be a man. Going through all that rigmarole of blusher, mascara, powder and lipstick every day? No thank you. I discovered another drawback to my new female identity when I realised I had nowhere to put my wallet and keys. There is, of course, always a handbag for this purpose, but that means you have to worry about putting the damn thing down everywhere. I decided that since Shirley had no pockets in the pink thing, stuffing my wallet and handkerchief into my underpants would have to do. Luckily, there is also no fine in Thailand for false advertising.

After my time in the make-up chair, I scrutinised my outfit. Without a doubt, I was the ugliest ladyboy that the world has ever clapped eyes on. Whereas Thai ladyboys are generally stunners in the beauty stakes, this *farang* ladyboy was stunningly awful. By this stage it was far too late to do anything different, so I hopped in the car and drove to the venue, which was on Pattaya Second Road, one of the main thoroughfares.

Parking was nearly impossible, but I did find a spot on the other side of the road, about 100 metres down. Checking I still had my wallet and handkerchief, in the privacy of my car I must add, I got out and began the walk to the pub.

One hundred metres in drag is a long way, and crossing a busy four lane road at 7 p.m. on a Saturday night is like one of those silly iron-man events where you swim, cycle and run for ever. Even the crossing itself was a sashay and stop, across each lane in turn. You can imagine what a commotion I caused in my hot pink outfit—aha, but you'd be wrong! There was no commotion, no honking of horns, no pointed fingers, no laughs of derision.

The drivers and passengers of Pattaya were content to just let this apparition be itself. If I wanted to be Shirley Bassey, it was 'up to me'. Where else would, or could this happen? Certainly not on London's Oxford Street, and though Sydney, Australia would welcome it at Mardi Gras you would be subject to a lot of laughs.

This story demonstrates what I said at the start, where else other than Thailand can you be left alone to just be yourself?

Thailand—a great place to die?

As Benjamin Franklin once said, 'In this world nothing can be said to be certain, except death and taxes.' This is a 100 percent certainty; unlike most things in life. If you stay in Thailand long enough, both the taxman and death will catch you up. Ex-pat residents have decided that Thailand is a great place to live, and I agree with this wholeheartedly. After 11 years, I have no regrets about choosing Thailand as my country of residence. However, I'm starting to think Thailand may not be such a great place to die.

Living in Thailand, we are subject to Thai law. What can or might happen in other countries may not be the norm in this country (like stopping at zebra crossings —Thais know there are no zebras crossing the road, so they don't have to slow for them). We are also living in a society that is predominantly Buddhist, so there is probably a greater importance given to 'life' than in the West. If you don't believe me, have you ever tried to have your cat or dog put to sleep? What is done in every veterinary clinic in the West is not done here. We are living in the mystic East; in instances like this it is impossible to forget this fact. It is almost well nigh impossible to have Fido helped towards his celestial kennel, unless you can find a Chinese vet.

Now let's look a little at our own impending demise (it's coming, so better get ready for it. The man in a raincoat is standing outside with the placard 'Prepare to meet thy doom!'). Most countries do not allow euthanasia, though it is not too difficult to have aggressive treatment withheld in the terminal situation. This is not the same in Thailand. Thai law and Thai medical ethics place an equally high importance on the maintenance of life, even with terminal cases. To not resuscitate someone with terminal cancer goes against Thai medical practice and belief.

Now I am not, in this book, going to debate the rights and wrongs of either side of the argument. The medical and legal philosophies between East and West are divergent, but I know what I want to happen to me in such a terminal situation. Or, rather, what I don't want to happen. I sure as hell don't want someone leaping on my chest and restarting my heart if I am terminal. I don't want to live for another week, or month, or whatever, with tubes in every available orifice, respirator breathing for me and nutrition being delivered via an intravenous line, while I am unable to communicate with the world. However, if you don't make these wishes known, before you are inexorably terminal, the above scenario is what will happen in Thailand.

It should also be pointed out that there was uproar in the UK many years ago when the sign DNR started appearing above hospital beds. As you probably know, this stands for 'Do Not Resuscitate' and is used to denote terminal cases. The doctors understood, but some relatives did not. People close to terminal patients live in hope that a medical miracle will save their loved ones. There is usually only a very faint chance of this, I'm afraid, even if you drink a gallon of Lourdes water every day. Your kidneys will be pleased, however.

The option of DNR is not as prevalent in Thailand as it is in the West. What, then, is to be done if this is your wish? What you have to do, is to make what is called a 'Living Will'. This is a medico-legal document, so you need to run it by your own legal person, and to be legal in Thailand, it must also be written in Thai, remember. The legality of opting for no aggressive intervention in your terminal phase lies in a universal Patient's Bill of Rights. This allows for patients to refuse medical treatment—but has to be done whilst they are of sound mind. When you arrive in ICU unconscious, it is a little late, and it can be argued that by that stage your soundness of mind is questionable.

Therefore it is very important to have your Living Will made out while you are still deemed to have your wits about you. In my hospital here, this document can be attached to your hospital notes, with a 'pop-up' advising the physicians that this document exists. If nothing else, this state your wishes, and (hopefully) the medical system will give it the requisite importance.

Please note that this Living Will is not a request for euthanasia. At no stage does it say anything about hastening your demise, but is merely a statement requesting the right to die as naturally as possible, and with dignity. Think about this and do some research via the internet. I would advise you to do something before you are terminal and unable to express your wishes coherently.

As an aside, it is important to note that although your significant other might be aware of your wishes and express them to the doctors, they will not be taken into account. The hospital can only act on your wishes, expressed by you, not by your wife or any other relative, before your impending demise. From the hospital's point of view, your wife could be looking at this from the financial angle of being the benefactor of your life insurance. It is not the institution's responsibility to guess anyone's real intentions.

Without being morbid, after our good friend Pascal Schnyder's father passed away, Som and I sat down and discussed what we wanted to happen when I finally get kicked off planet earth. I said, rather flippantly, that all I wanted was a private cremation with me and the man with the box of matches. I should have known better, Thailand's concept of departing is much more pragmatic than mine. I was informed by my good wife that when I die, I will have a Buddhist funeral, which will be held at Wat Nong Yai. The officiating monk will come from Wat Thammagai in Bangkok and prayers will be said to help me find my way to my next life. The unspoken inference was that I had not accumulated enough merit points to nick off to Nirvana this time around. Is there a place for us atheists, I wonder?

P.S. Yesterday I received a communication from a medical institute in Spain wanting me to collaborate with them on a research paper about the application of Living Wills in different countries. The implied promise was to have my name on scientific literature. Do I need this at my stage in life? I don't think so. I just need to remember to sign my Living Will and give it to the lovely ladies at the registration desk at the hospital. Have you done yours?

How I invented alternative fuels

Alternative fuels are today's buzzwords. It has come to the world's attention that the fossil fuel called crude oil is finite. We are going to run out of it very soon. There will be (are) shortages and with this comes queues at the pumps, and rising prices. This happens with any commodity where the demand starts to outstrip the supply. Like rice for example, which has doubled in price in 12 months, and as it is a staple good in Thailand it is causing financial headaches in the local population. In the past 12 months we have also seen the price of crude oil per barrel go over $140, more than doubling. The most exotic dish in the restaurants will soon be rice, lightly pan-fried in diesel. So what about next year? We must find an alternative, and soon.

The impetus propelling us towards alternative fuels is price. As the cost of gasoline goes up we look to see what else we can use. With the price of diesel remaining high (in fact higher than gasoline at the time of writing), the Thai government has been promoting petrol mixed with ethanol, called 'gasohol'. Gasohol is but one of these alternative fuels, as there is also LPG (Liquid Petroleum Gas) and CNG (Compressed Natural Gas), but gasohol is easier to get to the pumps, as it can be dispensed via a standard petrol bowser. Gasohol does not need to be stored under pressure in your car, so the chances of your fuel tank sending you into outer space is much less.

However, gasohol is not a new form of fuel. Gasohol first became of interest in 1979, with many discussions regarding its production and use in 1980. In 1985, its use was put forward in Thailand, so then gasohol is about 30 years old. Wrong! I date gasohol back to 1960.

Those of you who can, think back 50 years to the days of hardship before computers, ball point pens and cling-wrap. Gasoline was in plentiful supply, in fact in 1960, we expected fossil fuels to last for ever, just like plastic shopping bags. Gasoline was also very cheap, so why would anyone look to inventing the gasoline/alcohol mixture, which would become known as 'gasohol'? Surprise, surprise, the impetus was still cost, despite the cheapness and availability of gasoline. There were those who could not afford gasoline in 1960. I was one.

In 1960, I was the proverbial starving medical student. I had an 11-year-old car (an Austin A40) and lived in a cheap flat. My car represented two years of celibacy as women cost money (they did then as they still do now, even in Thailand) and the car was more important, having taken two years of scrimping and saving. There was only one problem; I did not have enough money left over after cornflakes to put petrol in it for the week. That reference to cornflakes is quite correct and has nothing to do with the prospect of sponsorship from Mr. Kellogg. It used to say on the side of the packet that one serving was the equivalent of one third of one's daily dietary requirements. You did not need to be Einstein (or have an electronic calculator, at that time not invented) to see that three bowls would get me through the day, no problem. Food was taken care of, but what about petrol?

The university provided the answer. I was forced to attend biochemistry classes once a week, and it was in the biochem laboratory I saw these huge carboys filled with crude petroleum and crude alcohol (don't ask me why they are called 'carboys' but apparently have been known as that since 1753, so don't say you didn't learn anything from this book!)

In my impecunious state, I suddenly saw salvation. It was one of those 'Eureka!' moments that would later change the entire history of the world. If I could get my car to run on a mixture of crude petroleum and crude alcohol, I had a free source of 'petrol' every Thursday.

The plan was hatched. Every Thursday I would park the A40 as close to the front door of the biochemistry lab as I could, and would remember my white lab coat. The pockets were large enough to carry one 500 ml flask in each, and it was a simple trip down the stairs to empty the flasks into the waiting Austin. For those of mathematical bent, that was one litre a trip, and I could manage many trips in a three hour practical class.

Those with a modicum of biochemical knowledge will know there is a problem here, as water is released when the two liquids are mixed. In fact, according to a text book I consulted just now, 'There is provided a process for making anhydrous alcohol denatured with gasoline for ready mixing with additional gasoline to make 'gasohol' and in which aqueous alcohol is introduced into a dehydration drying column along with gasoline.' Somehow, I knew this, but I did not have access to dehydration drying columns, but I did have access to 100 percent ether, which I knew could absorb the water. The final mixture that was laboriously dispensed and poured into my fuel tank had a 50:50 mixture of petroleum and alcohol with one litre of ether in every five litres of mixture. Thursday afternoons were very busy, filling 500 ml flasks, trotting down the stairs and keeping a record of how many flasks of each I had appropriated. My car ran, it could go one complete week on the biochem lab mixture, and I had, without knowing it at the time, invented 'Gasohol 50'.

During my research into this subject, I came across House Bill 322, of the State of Idaho, which stated 'The original definition of 'Gasohol' contemplated up to but no more than 10 percent anhydrous ethanol blended with gasoline. With the advent of advanced technological design, some vehicles being produced today can run on 85 percent ethanol blends. Burning this fuel (E85) in vehicles designed for use of E85 provides greater environmental air quality benefits than vehicles burning the 10 percent ethanol blends. Increased production of E85 vehicles and use of E85 fuel will provide benefits to air quality.'

So there you are gentle reader. Not only had I invented 'gasohol', but I was doing my bit towards making for a cleaner, greener planet. I could almost say I have saved the world (from what, I wonder). It is at times like this that I humbly feel that the gasohol manufacturers should be beating a path to my door, by way of thanks, and delivering a small token of their gratitude into my bank account. Numbers with several noughts after them should be ample recompense for using my 1960 invention and producing it commercially all these years later. I am sure you would agree. The Thai government could also throw in with my picture at the pumps, and a small royalty per litre. Please open your umbrellas as the flock of pigs passes overhead.

Driving in Thailand

One of the first things a *farang* notices when he first arrives in Thailand is the seemingly chaotic traffic. It seems at every intersection, there is a motorcycle lying on its side with a crowd of onlookers surrounding some bloodied rider and/or pillion passenger(s). Cars, buses and trucks thunder by at great speeds, and the sheer traffic volume far exceeds what you are used to. It's enough to make you turn around and flee back to the safety of speed cameras and traffic police.

A common question asked by new arrivals is, 'Do you really drive in this traffic?' This type of query is given even more weight when you find that many multinational companies operating in Thailand do not allow their ex-pats to drive and insist on providing Thai drivers. It then becomes quite a surprise when I inform the awestruck newbie that I do drive, and that it is actually easier to drive in Thailand than it was driving in Australia or the UK. Those who know of my motor racing background then retort, 'Yes, it's OK for you as you are used to danger and reckless driving, but what about the ordinary folk?'

Firstly, I should point out that in motor racing there are old drivers and bold drivers, but no old, bold drivers. Racing drivers are far from reckless. And neither are Thai drivers, though the opposite may appear to be true initially.

The main difference between driving in Thailand and driving in the West is the lack of aggression. Road rage is almost unheard of in Thailand. In western culture a horn is used to say, 'Get out of my way', a sounded horn in Thailand means, 'Please look out for me. I am here, please don't hit me!' I should also mention here the buses have very loud horns, which seem to be blown at random. Again these are not 'Get out of my way' warnings, but are questions to people standing on the pavement, 'Do you want to get on my bus?' The sounded horn, when returned by a waving arm from the pedestrian, sees the bus lurching into the left lane with the conductor leaning out of the door and waving his arm to warn the following traffic. Quaint, but it works.

Despite what it seems on the surface, Thai drivers are actually quite timid compared to those from the West. Four lanes on a highway can filter down into one without aggressive barging. Three lanes can get down into two without the traffic even appearing to slow, as drivers just make room for each other. Does this sound like Melbourne, Manchester or Manhattan? I doubt it.

Of course there is one very different aspect to driving in Thailand that you have to get used to very quickly, and that is the ubiquitous motorcycle. Typical of Asian cities, motorcycles are family transport, delivery vehicles and the ideal commuter chariot. I am waiting for some enterprising motorcycle manufacturer to begin advertising their new 125 cc step-through as 'The ideal motorcycle for a family of five.' Don't laugh; five on a motorcycle is commonplace. In fact you can buy an extra little saddle seat which fits in front of the main seat and is used for small children (who hang onto the rear vision mirrors), or the family dog, who just takes its chances. Mind you, a large percentage of the family pooches travel in the wire basket carrier at the front, cleverly blocking the headlights at night. Motorcycles are everywhere, though mainly in the left hand lane, but at the intersections they weave their way through the cars in all lanes to end up as a raucous pack at the front. This massed Moto-GP takes off, not when it's a green light, but at some point before the green, when the majority decide it is safe enough to go. Hence, the motorcycles lying on their sides in the middle of the intersection, having collided with vehicles playing 'last across' from the other direction. I mentioned in the first 'Farang' book—traffic lights in Thailand are only advisory, not compulsory.

Successful driving in Thailand does take a fair degree of observation skill; the majority of this is needed to look out for the dreaded two wheelers. This is comparable to the same observation skills used in the West to avoid speed cameras, red light cameras and plain clothes police cars, and other drivers with raging red mist in front of their eyes.

I could go on for days about the motorcycles. There is a saying here which goes: You know you've been in Thailand too long when you look both ways before crossing a one-way street. This is funny, but very true. Motorcycle riders will happily ride against the flow of traffic and smile and bob their head (usually without helmets) to say 'Thank you' as they thread their way through the streets. Motorcycles will also just poke their front wheels into an oncoming stream of cars until they either stop and let them out (because there is usually more than one), or run into them or into the oncoming traffic.

In the mornings, the motorcycles are people carriers. As I drive to work, I pass dozens of motorcycles and scooters with mothers at the handlebars and several children in school clothes perched behind and in front. Some are driven by the school children themselves. The children look as if they are only 10 years old but they are probably about 13. They ride with the flow of traffic and don't race each other or the cars, trucks and buses. I know that at 13 years of age if I had been given free reign to ride a motorcycle to school in this kind of traffic, my parents would not have had to worry about what to give me for my 14th birthday. I wouldn't have made it. I think this demonstrates some essential differences in the mental make-up of our different cultures.

The Thais are very inventive; this is evident in the unusual way they keep goods secure in transit. Instead of 'octopus' straps (also called bungy cords in some countries), they just use a pillion passenger. Consequently you will see a pillion passenger grasping a very large television set and hanging on, one assumes, by his anal sphincter. Paintings and large signs are also carried in this manner, but it will be held between rider and pillion across the seat of the motorcycle. The pillion cannot see where the rider is taking him/her and the wind tries to unseat him/her. The force of the wind is again, I imagine, countered by the aforementioned anal sphincter muscles.

There are some motorcycles which have been specifically modified to carry goods, and you will see a woman wobbling down the road towards you with two gigantic panniers, one each side and both carrying charcoal braziers (alight). Even the postman carries a load that would require at least one postal van in the West. Perhaps that might explain why so much mail gets lost in Thailand—it just blows away. Of course, let us not forget the motorcycle kitchen. These are three wheelers with a plastic sheet roof and a complete kitchen where the sidecar would be. This usually has a charcoal fire at one end for grilling. It will also be alight, showering charcoal sparks as it sputters down the road.

Farangs who plan to drive here need to be aware of some important 'rules' of the road. For example, when the approaching vehicle flashes its lights at you, this does not mean 'after you.' It means 'I am coming through.' More than one new driver has been surprised in this way. Turing on your hazard lights as you cross an intersection is another uniquely Thai system. This might be due to the view that it is a hazardous undertaking to cross an intersection but I have not seen this anywhere else. I still get confused by it as you wonder whether the vehicle is turning right or left or going straight on.

The final difference in driving in Thailand compared to commuting in the West is the result of the sheer volume of traffic. In Bangkok, for example, you will be lucky to exceed 40 kmh, and you spend huge amounts of time just sitting in traffic jams. Even on the overhead expressways where you can do 160 kmh at times, you will soon be brought back down to much slower speeds, if nothing else to stop at the pay station. Any attempts at high speed driving in the cities are useless at best and dangerous at worst. I drove Porsches in Australia averaging 160 kmh along the deserted roads of the outback, here in Pattaya I drive a dilapidated Daihatsu Mira. Its 850cc delivering anything but savage power and its blistering 80 kmh speed fits very well with the ebb and flow of Pattaya traffic.

I usually see one of my colleagues on the way to the hospital in the mornings. She drives a new BMW 5 Series. We arrive at the same time. Although she does have a more comfortable ride and enjoys a better sound system, she is no quicker.

While driving in Thailand may look impossible, in actual fact it is not. In some ways it is easier than in the West, though you do need to keep your peripheral vision as sharp as possible. And some motor vehicle insurance is a pretty good plan too.

2,000 monks, 30,000
locals and one atheist

When you marry a devout Buddhist, you have to be prepared for some give and take in the relationship. Where Buddhism has many celebrations and ceremonies, atheism cannot compete. Atheists do not hold ceremonies to celebrate the fact that they don't believe in something (or do believe in nothing). We don't even slaughter pigs to denounce vegetarianism. No, if it's pomp, circumstance, brass bands and wearing costumes, atheism isn't for you. When my wife asked me to join with the rest of the family in a huge merit-making ceremony at City Hall, I consented to go along. After all, if it was to be good for the family, I hadn't got much to lose, had I?

This particular ceremony was organised to provide assistance for the Buddhist temples in the south of Thailand, and was going to involve 2,000 monks. We would play a part in the proceedings by offering packets of food to the 2,000 saffron-robed monks. This began the night before, where we sat on the floor of the kitchen and began dispensing rice, sugar and garlic into small plastic bags. These were then sealed with rubber bands. I am led to believe more merit is gained this way, instead than just rushing down to the local supermarket and buying small packets of various foodstuffs.

I should mention at this stage that prowess with a rubber band seems to be on the Thai national school curriculum. Every Thai person knows how to twirl the bag of goodies and expertly snap the rubber band around the neck. Every Thai person also knows how to undo these rubber bands, while every *farang* I know ends up biting through the rubber bands in desperation, or spearing the thing with a fork.

My wife said that we should get up the next morning (Sunday) at 6 a.m. and go to the City Hall where the ceremony would take place. Knowing that the children would not be awake at 6 a.m. (and neither would their father), it was decided that 7 a.m. would be more satisfactory for this family I was told to wear something white, so I took a white shirt out of the wardrobe in preparation for the next day.

The next morning saw Som trying to get sleepy children dressed and organised, whilst her sleepy husband in his dazzling white shirt was detailed to load the car with several large plastic bags containing the bags of goodies. It was all systems go by 7.30 a.m. and we set off. As we approached City Hall, the road was blocked off, so I turned into a very small side street to try and get closer, via a back entrance. No such luck, as all access routes to City Hall were blocked. The friendly policeman suggested that we walk from where we were. We would not get any closer. So away we trudged, getting closer to the sound of cymbals and some joyful chanting. We could see the seated devout on both sides of North Road, streams of people ready to put offerings in the alms bowls of the 2,000 monks. North Road was covered in blue plastic sheeting for the residents dressed in white, while the monks would be walking up in single file, through the middle.

As we got even closer, school children came running up to help us carry the bags, and older kids directed us to a place on the blue plastic where we could wait with the others, for the monks to travel past us. Entrepreneurs snaked through the crowd selling large posters of the Buddha, whilst others were selling small tins of food for those who had come unprepared.

We sat in the sun and waited as the long procession of monks wound its way up to City Hall from the Dolphin Roundabout about two kilometres away. A very well organised fetch and carry system was in operation. When the alms bowls were filled, the contents were transferred to large sacks being carried by another army of young boys, and the now empty alms bowls began to be filled once more. Eventually the monks reached us and the children had a wonderful time putting our small bags of offerings into the never ending stream of monastic begging bowls, until our large carry bags were empty. These in turn were collected by another army of young workers, and in no time at all, North Road was returned to vehicular transport.

I was aware of the fact that a large number of people had turned out for this religious event, but I had not any idea of the true numbers until I read the *Pattaya Mail* the following Friday.

I quote from the paper: 'Local residents gathered to offer food to 2,000 monks and novices on August 10, making merit for the occasion of Her Majesty the Queen's birthday and for the support of 266 Buddhist temples in the troubled Southern provinces. With over 30,000 people gathering on North Pattaya Road between City Hall and the Dolphin Roundabout, starting from 6a.m., it was believed to be the largest Buddhist ceremony ever held in Pattaya. Phra Kru Wijitr Thamasarn, head abbot of Banglamung District, led the monks, while Mayor Itthipol Khunplome led the laymen, most of the latter being dressed in white.

'This time of the year, in the rainy season, is regarded by devotees as being particularly important to offer food to the monks, who by tradition are not allowed to leave their temples. August 12 is also National Mother's Day, the birthday of Her Majesty, and Buddhists throughout Thailand make merit by offering food and essentials to the monks.

'This year there has been enormous concern for the 266 temples in the troubled provinces of the South, where the monks cannot gather food, resulting in special supplies having to be sent to them. Mayor Itthipol delivered a speech in both Thai and English, and the ceremony in which people donated both food and money lasted about two hours.'

I can forgive the newspaper's reporter for overlooking the one atheist, but by forgiving him, I suppose I am allowing him to pick up any merit points I might have earned that Sunday. '*Anumotana.*'

World peace and bouncy castles

Whilst *farangs* in Thailand are definitely in a minority, they do more than their fair share when it comes to charity. The foreign residents show their appreciation of their adopted homeland by supporting many, many charities for Thailand's needy and underprivileged. One of these is the Jesters Care for Kids in Pattaya, which has raised over 38 million baht for local children.

As a concerned *farang*, although I have never been involved in the organisation of the charity, I have been involved. If you like to go to the website (www.care4kids.com) you will read the following entry. '1998 —counting the proceeds the next morning we realised we made the million baht mark by the skin of our teeth. Many insiders believe we were able to achieve that goal with the shocking auction bid of 24,000 baht for the infamous 'Full Monty' photo of four unspecified members of the Jesters.' This is where I came in. I was the photographer for the famous photo, which we took in a piece of scrubland on the top of Phra Tumnak Hill about 9 p.m. one night. By the way, it could hardly be described as even 'soft' porn (perhaps ultra-soft) as all the Jesters were holding their crash helmets in front of their dangly bits.

That was the first major attempt at fundraising in Pattaya and everyone wondered if 1998's total could be raised in 1999. The local populace did respond and 1.4 million baht went into the coffers.

By 2000 that year's figure reached two million baht, and it has continued to climb since then, now attracting many corporate sponsors. I spoke to 'Woody' Underwood from the Jesters in August 2008 and the charity had at that point raised over 38 million baht. That's a lot of care for a lot of kids.

Being a Southeast Asian country, Thailand does have its (un)fair share of beggars. They increase in the high season and you will see waifs sitting in the gutter with an empty proffered cup, which is usually from McDonalds. Do more beggars eat at McDonalds than any other fast food takeaway, I wonder?

The answer to this and all other questions about Thailand can be found by reading either the *Pattaya Mail* or the *Chiang Mai Mail's* favourite Agony Aunt, called Hillary. This redoubtable spinster has been answering all kinds of questions for over a decade, but remains very reclusive, becoming even more so, as she ages. With the kind permission of the *Pattaya Mail*, here is one of her seekers of advice, and her reply:

'Dear Hillary,

This one is a bit different from the usual ones you get here. What is your advice on beggars? Should you, or shouldn't you? I find them at all the overbridges and the ones with obvious physical disabilities or young babies are difficult to walk past. But I am told that my concern is misplaced as they aren't real beggars at all. What do you suggest, as I do not want to appear stingy, as I am reasonably well off, but I certainly do not want to be ripped off either.

Bob

Dear Bob,

Always a difficult question, and one that foreigners here have a problem with all the time. You are generous by nature, and understand that there can be great differences in wealth. However, your pockets are probably nowhere near as deep as the pockets of some of the members of the Thai community, and you will not often see them donating to waifs at the roadside. There are much better ways of distributing largesse and this is through the service clubs and organisations. This way, your donation goes directly to where it is needed, and nothing is skimmed off the top for "middle men". So my suggestion is to certainly put something into charity, but do it through people like the Jester's Care 4 Kids or the Ploenchit Fair, or through Rotary, Lions and other groups such as the Pattaya Charity Club or the Yasothon school project run by Norman and Eileen Denning (Yorkies).'

So, returning to the Jester's Children's Fair, one of the most enjoyable experiences in Pattaya, as children, rich and poor come to enjoy all the rides and activities. After one of the Children's Fairs, I wrote the following for the *Pattaya Mail*.

'My two and a half year old Marisa [as she was then], is now just big enough to enjoy the activities, though obviously one of the younger ones, and it was while watching her at the Bouncy Castle, that something really struck me. There were around thirty children, of ages from my Marisa upwards to young teenagers, of many different nationalities, colours and creeds, all playing there.

'Not only playing, but helping each other get up after a tumble, laughing together and looking out for each other. A multinational, multicultural mix of children that could show us adults what we seem to be unable to do. Work, live and play in harmony.

'If we adults could only act with friendliness towards each other on the 'bouncy castle' of Mother Earth, our planet would be a much better place on which to live.'

If children can live in harmony when adults can not, there is a message there for everyone. Why are we breeding distrust of others and hate into our children? It is not something that comes naturally. Could ideology and dogma be the culprits? Or is it a responsibility that all we adults have to shoulder?

Sometimes I fear for the human race. Our children are handling society much better than we are. How sad.

Education in Thailand

My daughter was four years old when I wrote this. She could speak English and Thai fluently, Laos (Isaan) for fun and Chinese when prompted. At the same time, her little brother Evan was then two and a half, and could understand both English and Thai and speak one or two word sentences in either language, and what he didn't know he could make up. He also knows a little Chinese (and that's not Ah Wong from the Chinese takeaway on the corner).

It would be gratifying to think that Som and I had produced a couple of child prodigies. Somehow the mix of Thai and western chromosomes had produced today's answer to Albert Einstein, but that would be far too ego inflating, as well as being erroneous.

The answer is (as well as being raised in a bilingual environment) in the education system that can be tapped into in Thailand. You see, by the time she was four, Little Miss Marisa had been going to school for two and a half years and Little Mister Evan for 12 months.

Yes, children can go to 'school' from 18 months of age. The entry level for children at this age means that the teachers have to be adept at both keeping an eye on explorative toddlers and at changing dirty nappies. I don't care how much they might offer me in salary; I'm not changing some other child's crappy nappy. I have been known to take our children out into the garden, hose them down and bury the offending, and offensive, nappy in the flower bed.

So here we have our son, who has now 'graduated' from nursery level to a full-blown Kindergarten kid, and here's his school timetable. Don't forget that he is two and a half years old.

Every day he starts with grammar and then on to his Chinese lessons. Then it is Thai or English, depending upon the day, followed by a 10 minute break. Suitably refreshed after a bottle of yoghurt milk he then has more English or PE or swimming followed by general knowledge and maths, cooking, moral education or art. And that's only till lunch and a lie down. I'd need a lie down after all that too.

After being prodded awake after lunch it is into creative activities and more art and he finishes with music and movement. After looking at that timetable, I don't blame him for not wanting to do his homework when he comes home. And he's just two and a half, the age when you and I were looking at Noddy and Big Ears on the box, without a care in the world, other than wondering where and what time the next meal was going to be. Those, of course, were the days before we found out that Noddy was gay and you're not allowed to make fun of people with big ears. We have come such a long way, haven't we?

However, whilst I think that looks fairly formidable, I cannot say that the children feel the same. Little Mister is dressed and ready to go by 7.30 a.m., cursing his big sister for being such a sleepy head and slowing them down. If he is late for school he gets very upset, whilst Marisa doesn't worry too much, but then she's in Kindergarten Two, so it's all old hat for her, being a 'senior' student if you please.

Looking at it all dispassionately, the children are not complaining, mother gets time off from child rearing, and they do learn some useful skills, though I wonder just how much moral education gets through to someone who is two and a half years old? Evan, in particular, needs a parental wallop on the backside every so often to remind him of such things as proprietary rights. However, it does seem like a win-win situation. Other than for my wallet, as this private education is not cheap, being 60,000 baht each per year (which is in the lower bracket of private school fees, by the way). This can be converted to roughly 1,000 pounds each, which would still be a lot less expensive than private education in the UK or Australia—but of course income is correspondingly less in Thailand.

Now that is private education, but the same standards cannot be applied to public schooling in

Thailand. Education for the average Thai child does not encompass all the subjects taught at private schools, and the English language, in particular, is not as well taught as in the Philippines, India, Malaysia or Singapore. Even in government schools, there are school fees which have to be met, notwithstanding the much vaunted 'free' education to year 12, and although these fees are only something like 1,500 baht a term, plus books and uniforms, this can be a hardship for the poorer families. You only have to see the queues at the government run pawnshops the week before school starts again, to understand just how hard it can be. And yet the average Thai family believes that it is only through education that the children will be able to raise themselves (and their parents) from the dirt poor level, and are willing to sacrifice everything towards that end.

However, that same poor family is not getting the best education according to such gurus as Dr. Ko-Chih Tung from one of the UNESCO units. He was reported in the *Bangkok Post*'s education supplement this year (2008) discussing the Thailand government schooling as saying, 'When it comes to content of education it's less than satisfactory.' He went on to say, 'the content does not reflect the needs of a country that should be growing and developing into the international community. It is as though it is an assimilation education [designed to] preserve the status quo.'

Dr. Tung concluded by saying, 'If you look at the curriculum, there's a lot of emphasis on morality, ethics and social studies, etc., but there's no serious attention to science, technology, mathematics and the creative part. So that's why I give Thailand low grades, in fact less than satisfactory. In contrast, the private education system in Thailand—which is a western-oriented education—teaches confirmative education.'

Even those children whose parents can easily send them to the government school can be further disadvantaged, more than just curriculum matters. Many of the schools are in dreadful need of repair, in fact, there is one in Yasothon in the North-East that is so dilapidated, a group of *farangs* is raising money to build a new one. Eileen and Norman Denning run a small guest house and butchery in Jomtien, and are in the process of raising the 1.5 million baht necessary to do this. Despite the much vaunted mega projects being mooted by the government, the charities supported by the *farang* community are numerous. By the way, I am not implying that the Thai community does not look after their own disadvantaged; they do, and are also unsung heroes.

There is another group of children in Thailand which has an even greater problem as far as schooling is concerned. These are children without papers. Only registered Thai children are eligible for a place in a government school. No papers, no place. So the children of refugees, hill tribes children and those of illegal immigrants from Laos, Cambodia and Burma cannot go to school, thus nullifying any chance of betterment of themselves and their families.

Fortunately there are charities, generally run by western religious orders such as the Sisters of Mercy, who go and pick up these 'non-Thai' children and bring them to their schools where they are bathed, fed and educated, then run home again in the afternoons, home being a packing case beside a public dump in many instances. Thailand may have a wealthy upper class, but it also has a huge number of disadvantaged families, and ones that are non-citizens don't even make it into the statistical charts.

After those previous paragraphs showing the downside of education, there is however more than a glimmer of hope. And that is the adult education. A large number of young Thais drop out of school for many reasons, usually financial—the student being required to go to work to assist the family budget being one of the principal reasons. However, there is a state run Sunday school adult education, whereby young adults can attend and eventually matriculate, allowing them to go on to university.

My wife Som is one of those, dutifully getting dressed in the compulsory (tight) white shirt and black skirt, leaving the children with me on the Sunday morning. The wife of a friend of mine has done this so successfully she is now studying to be a lawyer at one of the universities, so it is possible for someone to rise above the mediocrity implied by UNESCO's Dr. Tung. I look at Som and her classmates as perhaps the hope of Thailand in the future.

Finally, there are certainly excellent private educational opportunities in Thailand, all the way through to International Baccalaureate (IB) levels, but for the children, it helps if they choose their parents wisely. Marisa and Evan will thank us one day. In any one of their four languages will do. By the way, the Laos comes from Nanny.

Releasing fish

It was Som's birthday this week and the main beneficiary was around 10 kg of catfish. Let me explain all this a bit better.

What you have to first understand is that birthdays do not have the same significance to Thai people as they do to us westerners. In fact, the supposed date of birth can be out by many years. What happens, up in the country villages, is that when the child is eventually registered, that date is taken as the date of birth, or alternatively, the uncle who has gone to the *amphur* office to do the registration (before the child goes to school) has a guess, and that's it. In Som's case, we 'know' her date of birth is at least two years wrong, and forget about the day and month. However, for us, her birthday is taken to be 2 October, and we will forget about the year. Most women will understand that aspect!

For Som, her birthday is more of a reminder to get some merit points in the celestial merit bank, as each year she will make the pilgrimage to her favourite temple in Bangkok (Wat Thammagai) and comes home all bright-eyed and tells me she has got lots of merit for me, which I get after repeating *anumotana*. Which particular bank is counting all these merit points for this atheist, I am unsure, but I'm sure some good will come out of it, somewhere, sometime.

As well as the trip to the temple, Som likes to release fish, which would have otherwise ended up lying beside some chips and covered in batter. This fish salvation is a family affair, and we all go to the fresh food market and find the fish stalls. When I say 'fresh' food, I mean it. Large tubs of fish are all flapping around, and when you make your choice, the fish stall will also fillet, gut and scale your previously live purchase. This is done by Muslim traders, as it would be very bad karma for a Buddhist to do this. But for us, they remain whole and very alive.

In the back of the car we have a large plastic tub for the purchased fish, and as usual, we cleaned out the fishmonger's stock. This time it only cost us about 500 baht for around 10 kg of fish, and away we sped towards the Wat Yarn temple complex, about 10 km from home. This is set around a large lake and is a very picturesque setting.

So with the four of us lugging the plastic tub, (Som, me and the two children) we descend the steps from one of the temple salas, to the water, and with silent prayers ceremoniously tip the fish into the lake.

I have to say that the fish really were appreciative, with some of them doing dolphin impersonations, skimming along the surface and jumping for joy. I suppose that if I were a just released catfish, I might have done the same.

However, this time was slightly different. On the way home I heard a commotion in the back of the car and when I opened the boot, there was one not so bright catfish which had obviously jumped out of the tub on the way to the temple.

Speaking to it severely, and telling it never to do that again, we found a little stream close to home and told him that would have to do, and *anumotana* for him. I hope he made it to somewhere safe, though I have this sneaking suspicion he is going to end up in beer batter in a frying pan. In the interim, I will refrain from ordering fish and chips.

To mark the event in western fashion, I did bring home a cake, complete with inscription done at no extra charge by the bakery. I thought that 'Happy Birthday Mummy' would go down well with the children, who had roundly enjoyed their own birthday cakes this year, complete with blowing out the candles.

As Evan had three candles and Marisa had four, it was decided that Mummy should have six (isn't children's mathematics wonderful). They were lit, and the children combined to blow them all out. It was then that I saw the inscription 'Happy Birthday Mummmy', but whatever, it was nicely done. English was not the first language for the young girl in the cake shop.

Again, thinking in *farang* mode, I was going to suggest that we go out to dinner at a swanky restaurant, but no. Som had invited a couple of the ladies from our village, and they happily sat together on the floor of the kitchen pounding chillies into a red sludge, to be added to all the other ingredients to make an Isaan *Som Tum*.

The party for the ladies was then held on our porch, seated on the mat reserved for eating. Isaan food only tastes good when eaten from the floor. That much I have learned. They chatted till all hours sipping the weakest blended scotch and cola until they had run out of drinks and mixers and the mat was folded up for another day.

Another 'birthday' milestone had been passed, and the trip to the Bangkok temple will be on Sunday, and she will return fully regenerated, spiritual batteries fully charged. It's a simple life in some ways, but a personally fulfilling one as well. However, I will be celebrating my birthday at Casa Pascal's, complete with a bottle of Veuve Clicquot.

No thanks, Pascal, 'I won't have the fish this time!'

Footnote: Som's favourite soothsayer has told her that if I release fish on my birthdays, I will live to be 100. He did not say how long the fish will live.

Bob the builder

Thailand is a growing country, where new buildings are popping up at an amazing rate. Over the years I have watched Thappraya Road between Pattaya and Jomtien change from being a single track to two lanes to what will shortly be a six lane bitumen highway. Mind you, the last transition is still in progress as I write this, and has been in progress for around two years. Progress is not done to a measured beat here—fits and starts is a better description of what goes on.

There have been new shops built on both sides of the road. Six years ago there were only a few buildings like Ib and Kannikar Ottesen's Residence Suites and their Residence Gardens (where I celebrated my wonderful 60th birthday). In some ways, that was the beginning, as now both sides of Thappraya Road are fully lined with buildings.

Initially, we (the wise ones) said, 'Where are all the people going to come from to buy these shophouses?'

To the western mind, this was an economic disaster about to unfold before our disbelieving eyes. But we were wrong. Around 90 percent of the shophouses now have tenants and there are even new hotels built on the road, such as Steve Graham's Nirvana Place at the top of the hill. You might be wondering what economic miracle enabled this to happen.

There is no miracle, just Thai pragmatism, as it was all explained to me by my wife Som (a walking example of the aforesaid pragmatism). The occupants of all the new buildings are not new owners, but merely tenants. The families that move into the shophouses are not looking to make large profits from their commercial enterprises. They are really just looking for enough money to cover the rents, whilst the rest of the family goes out to earn the money to live, brought in through their monthly salaries.

This family enterprise has then 'free' accommodation, plus one, two or more incomes each month, depending upon the size of the family living there. The family that stays together pays together.

This sociological model does work. It worked for all the Greek immigrants who came to Australia in the postwar boom, and who now own shopping malls and their sons and daughters are professionals like doctors and lawyers. The Thai model is perhaps 50 years behind the Aussie-Greek one, but it is happening. The family unit will be the winner.

But I have strayed from my original concept by getting deep and philosophical. Back to the real world, and the building trade in particular. On every building site you will see labourers working away at the measured pace of the Thai.

Whilst we are used to the pace of western building, it does not work here. In an ambient temperature of 30 degrees Celsius and above, your average worker is not going to work at a European pace. In fact, you may find that there are two people doing what you would consider a job for one.

If I were to put a label on Thai building construction, it would be 'near enough is good enough'. The operating principle is, if the corner's angle is only 88 degrees instead of 90 degrees, does it really matter? If the roof has a fall of two degrees instead of being exactly level, does it really matter?

Now, we *farangs* place an enormous importance on geometric purity in building, but the Thais do not. Their belief is that a building should have four sides and a roof and keep out the (majority of the) rain. What more do you need?

I know of one *farang* having his house built, who kept on coming around with spirit levels and surveyor's tape and insisting that walls be knocked down and rebuilt to exactly 90 degrees. Will his house last any longer than the one next door? I doubt it, but the foreigner obviously sleeps well with his feet perfectly aligned with the walls.

This is one of the reasons that many foreigners will only buy houses where the project manager is also a foreigner. 'European standards' is the catch-cry.

But is it really? Many foreign project managers were never project managers in their own countries, but were probably electricians, or plumbers, or with some luck even a brickie. 'Near enough is good enough' if a foreigner signs it off. Cement render can cover a multitude of sins.

I have personal experience of the cement render technology. I came home one day to find Som with a bucket of cement and a pile of those crazy half-size Thai bricks, making little walls around her garden beds. I christened this project The Great Wall of China, but she successfully completed it with a three brick high enclosure around the plants and palm trees she had planted in our garden. That wasn't the end of the matter. The tenant across the road had requested that his back wall be made one metre higher to keep out unwanted dogs (of which Thailand has several million). I suggested to Som that we get a local builder in to do this job.

'No, I will do it,' said my wife.

Whilst I had previously acknowledged that the Great Wall of China was indeed a masterpiece, this was an entirely different situation. This wall was around 50 metres long and one metre high. Time for real builders, said I.

'No, I can do it,' Som persisted, 'I watched them building the walls at the house next door.'

What has to be understood here is that there is no real apprenticeship system as in the UK or Australia or Europe. You just join a work gang and pick it up from there. When you hire someone they could have started on the brickie career path that very day. He was a motorcycle taxi rider last week, and probably will be a dishwasher in McDonald's the week after.

There are vocational courses run by the government that are divided into five major fields: agriculture, home economics, business studies (marketing, travel and tourism, public relations), arts and crafts, and technology (mechanical, civil, electronic, industrial).

You will not see bricklaying in that list. Some vocational schools and technical colleges do, however, offer a one year programme leading to the Tradesman Certificate. This programme is offered to students who have completed lower secondary school and prepares them for immediate employment upon graduation.

That's the theory, but the reality is there are so many positions available in the building industry, why would you wait for 12 months before you start? And a further reality is that the European project manager is overseeing unskilled, or partially skilled Thai builders. You have to feel sorry for both sides.

So Som, a.k.a. Bob the Builder, began work on the back wall. Sand and gravel were delivered by the local building supplies, along with large concrete bricks. String lines were put in place and the work continued in between dropping off and picking up children from school and cooking dinner. I have to admit that she did an excellent job, and the imperfections were easily covered by the aforementioned cement render.

Another triumph for Thai industriousness? Another triumph for the tenacity of Thai women? Or just another brick in the wall, as Pink Floyd's Roger Waters told us all in 1979.

An accidental meeting (or three)

In a previous chapter I wrote about driving in Thailand, and how it is necessary to have eyes in the back of your head, challenge all red lights as being liars and turn your motorcycle detector to the maximum level.

Despite all my sage advice, I have managed to have the odd accident or three, and unfortunately, these were not great experiences. For some ex-pats these accidents have been enough for them to decide to leave the Kingdom. I can see how this might be the case, after my last experience I was harbouring quite a lot of negative thoughts myself. After I put it into perspective, however, I was able to calm myself down.

The first accident occurred when I was turning right coming out of a side street. I stopped, looked in both directions and proceeded. As I did so, I suddenly saw a motorcycle with two people on board crossing my nose. Bump and down they went. Since I was travelling barely above crawling speed, the impact was slight and

I stopped immediately. The motorcycle was on its side just in front of my car, the rider (male) was getting up from the ground, but the pillion passenger (female) just lay there motionless. They were also surrounded by an empty plastic container and a week's worth of dirty laundry.

I immediately went to the aid of the woman, who quickly regained consciousness. Later I have found that 'fainting on demand' is a skill possessed by all Thai women.

The man had an abrasion to his right knee, but was otherwise fine. Of course, neither of them could speak English, and since I could speak even less Thai than I do now, I knew we were going to have severe communication problems. The local policeman arrived, and drawing a spray can of enamel, traced the outline of my car and their motorcycle on the road. After he did this, he told me I should take the rider to hospital to be checked out. By this stage, I had managed to contact a Thai friend who also told me that I should take the chap to hospital, and since I was a foreigner I should pay for the medical treatment.

Since I was in a reasonable degree of shock myself, I agreed and a passing *song taew* was hailed. The injured man and I were taken to the most expensive private hospital in the area. This is another acceptable result of accidents between foreigners and locals. A hospital that the injured Thai could never afford to go to becomes his birthright after close encounters of the *farang* kind. Only when the *farang* is paying, of course.

Paying for treatment was a breeze compared to what was to come. This next item was the most chilling. Under Thai law, if the effects of the injury last more than 21 days, then the accident is deemed to be a criminal case and if the *farang* is found guilty (which he will be), the subsequent penalty includes deportation. My motorcycle rider had his wound dressed, told to come back in one week, and was then given a certificate to excuse him from work for three weeks. This put me right in the deportation danger zone.

The day of horrors was not over yet. Mr. Motorcycle and I then had to go to the police station where I had to surrender my car keys and my passport. Then came the slow and laborious statements. Being Thailand, and as this was becoming a legal case, the reports had to be in Thai. As the policeman was barely literate in my native tongue, we had a problem, until a young secretary sat with the policeman and relayed my English testimony into Thai. How accurately this was done, I have no idea, but I had to sign the document and was then dismissed to return in one week. I was also told to advise my insurance company and give them the police report.

I duly returned after one week, with a bilingual Thai friend, and I was told that I had to take the injured man back to the hospital and pay for his review. This time I had my Thai friend relay the fact to the treating doctor that the certificate should be less than twenty-one days, and fortunately he agreed to amend it to twenty days. I was certainly not out of the woods yet and could see myself at the exit gate if things did not start to go my way. Another week later we repeated the rigmarole and returned to the policeman's office afterwards. It was at this meeting that another Thai characteristic became apparent. My motorcycle rider was in line for an Oscar for his exaggerated limp which had appeared between the hospital and the police station.

Fortunately the insurance company sent a representative to this meeting and much deep discussion ensued between all the parties concerned, except me. Put yourself in this scenario. Your future is being earnestly discussed and you do not know what they are saying, but every so often there is mention of large sums of money, several thousands in fact.

The upshot was for the meeting to reconvene in six days, when I would know if I had to start packing. It was not a fun time, but eventually we all assembled in the policeman's office. The insurance company had sent another representative who had a good command of English and the scene unfolded in front of me.

It seemed my injured motorcyclist wanted 60,000 baht, or else he would have to stay off work for another two weeks, and thus make me a criminal in the eyes of Thai law. The insurance company was prepared to go to 30,000 baht but no more. We were at an impasse.

There were more negotiations in Thai and then a hurried *sotto voce* asked me would I put a 'sweetener' of 20,000 baht on top of the insurance payout? By this stage I was ready to sell my grandmother into slavery to get out of this mess. I agreed.

This was imparted to the aggrieved injured who then agreed and there were large smiles all round. I was *wai'd* to and made to feel that this was garnering me much merit, even though it was cleaning out my piggy bank. The way to eternal salvation was obviously paved with broken piggy banks, especially if you are a *farang*.

I was given time to run up to the closest ATM and make the withdrawal, and my friend informed me we were not finished with the handouts yet.

'Put some money in an envelope for the policeman,' I was told. 'And something for the insurance man.'

I returned and the 20,000 was ceremoniously given to the insurance representative who in turn gave it to the motorcycle rider, who was remarkably much improved after the financial salve. So much so that he was able to easily walk to his motorcycle and kick it into life. Buddha be praised. After this and after I handed the police and insurance men their 'donations', I was given my passport and the keys to my car, and was a free man again.

That was many years ago, when I had only been here for three months. These days I am a lot savvier, and understand the system. There are no insurmountable problems, just financial settlements. The skill is in organising settlements that are not financially debilitating. This is best done through your friendly insurance broker. There have, of course, been some minor scrapes with other motorcycles since then. I was always able to smile and offer the odd 1,000 baht note to cover a minor touch-ups and everyone would smile and drive / ride away in our separate directions, with my wallet only slightly lightened. That was until last year, when I sinned again.

I was coming home and crossing a suburban road. I looked down to my right and it seemed to be clear. Three quarters of the way across I suddenly saw a motorcycle coming at me on the wrong side of the road; he was unable to stop and gently bumped my front mudguard. The rider was about 10 years of age and his pillion, his little brother, was around eight. Neither was hurt, although the rider had twisted his ankle and was limping slightly. (In retrospect, I wonder if they have limping lessons in the Thai school curriculum.) Getting out of my car, I forgot all about '*jai yen*' and my *farang* indignation boiled over. I had been run into by a damn 10-year-old who could have no license and on the wrong side of the road. This was not my fault. I forgot all about the '*farang* pays' rule. This stems from the ingrained concept in Thailand that if the *farang* hadn't been there, the accident would never have happened.

Since I ignored their demands that I pay for the (slight) damage to the motorcycle, the police, an ambulance and tow truck quickly arrived. There was no need for any of these new arrivals, but my stupidity was causing the situation to develop. I got down from my high horse, rang the insurance company and within 30 minutes their representative arrived and everything was smoothed over. For a paltry 5,000 baht the parents of the 'injured' boy were appeased, the policeman forgot about the fact that the boy was underage, the ambulance and tow truck left the scene and everyone was happy again. That is, everyone except me.

I should have kept my cool, smiled and apologised a lot, and looked as if I was interested in the welfare of the boy. Then, if I had given the parents 1,000 baht I would have been away and home in time for tea. There are ways of doings things in Thailand which must be followed, at the risk of your own (financial) peril. Never forget, we *farangs* will always be aliens in a foreign land.

The state of emergency

Have I now done everything? As well as living through a coup in the first 'Farang' book, I have now watched a red-shirted insurgence, been up close to a riot policeman and endured a state of emergency. Of course, along with all this, I have remained in an area where western governments advised their populace not to visit, as it is too dangerous.

Have I been brave in the face of enemy action? Should I receive the George Cross for civilian courage? No, but I did get a cup of coffee from Paulo Randone, the GM of the dusit D2 baraquda hotel (sorry, but that's the way they spell the name of the hotel.)

An explanation of Thai politics might be needed at this point. Thailand is attempting to become a democracy, and the very word 'democracy' is bandied about by all parties in the Thai political arena as if it were the holy grail. However, like the aforementioned grail, Thailand is still seeking this elusive democracy.

Sure, elections are held every couple of years or so (with a coup or two in between), and they are welcomed by the poor and socially disadvantaged. Not welcomed because they give the ordinary Thai citizen the chance to shape the country, but welcomed with an open piggy bank as the vote buying machine deposits around 500 baht into each voter's impoverished budget. This is, of course, denied in some quarters, but proven vote buying managed to bring down a political party last year and exclude some of its members for five years. This method of electioneering is well entrenched in Thai society, and is the accepted 'democratic' method, even for the *'kamnan'* (village head) elections. As a concept, it works at village level, but hardly represents real democracy and its Westminster style government that Thailand aspires to having.

Thaksin Shinawatra, one of the richest men in Thailand, was then well placed to assure himself of victory in the polls, being well versed in the business concept of 'if you don't speculate, you can't accumulate'.

But a coup ensued, ousting Thaksin who went to the UK and bought a football club.

Having set the political background, now let us look at what happened at the end of 2008 and again at the end of the first quarter of 2009, when I met my riot policeman.

The pressure group opposing the Thaksin Shinawatra nominee government had adopted wearing yellow shirts, and began concerted acts of civil disobedience. This culminated in the peaceful sit-in at Bangkok's Suvarnabhumi international airport which precipitated the end of that Thaksin backed government. This colourful concept was not new, however, as in 184 C.E. the peasants rose up against the government and identified themselves by wearing yellow turbans. However that was in China, not Bangkok. Our one came much later and the yellow anti-Thaksin group called themselves the People's Alliance for Democracy, or the PAD.

Of course, this in turn brought out a group in favour of the deposed PM and his fallen governments who then wore red shirts and called themselves the United Front for Democracy Against Dictatorship, which somehow became the acronym UDD. Since the PAD appeared to have won their point with civil disobedience, the red-shirted UDD could see that this was going to be the answer to getting their desires as well.

Organised sit-ins at Parliament House became the norm in Bangkok, but were not really having the impact the UDD wanted. With the ASEAN Summit going to be held in Pattaya, this presented a wonderful opportunity for extreme civil disobedience, and for the red shirts, another opportunity for a 500 baht note, free lunch and new shirt. Yes, make no mistake about this, both the yellows and the reds were guilty of currying favours financially.

On the Saturday morning of the summit, I drove into my office in town, and there were trucks with red-shirted banner wavers for several city blocks, having come down from Bangkok, plus 100 taxis. It was *Songkran* without the water. Everyone was having a helluva good time.

After parking the car I walked to my usual Saturday morning breakfast venue on Second Road, and there, lining the street outside the dusit D2 baraquda was a platoon of riot police with plexiglass shields, truncheons, funny hats with fan-shaped protection at the nape of the neck and foreboding black shirts and pants and bovver boots.

It would be gilding the lily to say they were on full alert, as most of them were sitting on the kerb smoking cigarettes, but I suppose they were ready for something, but nobody had told them what the something was. I found out later that the New Zealand group were supposed to be staying at the D2, but they hadn't arrived yet. Ah well, be prepared as the Boy Scouts used to say.

But the real action was at the other end of town, where the Summit venue was in the grounds of the Royal Cliff Beach Resort, a property with only one road access, which could have been blocked by two trucks and half a dozen determined men. OK, make that a dozen.

Just to make sure, the police and the army were also on guard, suitably kitted out in all the repellant attire, and numbered around 2,000. That should have been more than enough, but of course it wasn't. What has to be remembered is that ex-PM Thaksin came from the ranks of the police, and many of their number were closet red shirts. With Thailand politically polarised, it was a fair bet that under some of the army uniforms there lurked the odd red shirt or two as well.

The mob, alias the red shirts, now suitably fuelled with rhetoric and probably copious quantities of *lao khao* (rice whiskey), just marched through the 'defenders', smashing the glass doors to the convention hall and running amok, causing damage as they went. Mobs are not well known for putting everything neatly back in its place. In fact, the damage bill was later found to be around 14 million baht (300,000 pounds Sterling), not an inconsiderable sum.

The summit was naturally called off and the delegates left by helicopter as the roads were still a sea of red shirts, internationally embarrassing the government of Abhisit Vejajjiva. The riot police outside the D2 put out their cigarettes and dispersed, and returned to Bangkok.

The red shirts also returned to Bangkok, celebrating and thinking they had won their fight to topple the government and carried on with mob violence in a small area of the capital, commandeering buses to use as barricades, and attempting to storm government house again.

But they hadn't won. The citizens of Bangkok were also mightily sick of this interruption to their normal living and began to fight back. Just so the others knew who was who, the residents donned blue shirts. Thailand is a colourful nation!

With the government declaring a state of emergency, a more determined police and army then routed the

2,000 dissidents with tear gas and water cannon and the UDD leaders surrendered. It was all sort of anti-climactic but order was restored.

What has to be remembered is that 2,000 red shirts in a city of 10 million, give or take two million and a similar number of dogs, does not bring the city to a halt. The noodle sellers continued selling noodles, the bar girls continued gyrating around chrome poles and the other 9.8 million inhabitants carried on as usual, other than those who worked in the hotel and hospitality industry, as the foreign governments had issued travel warnings and some press had headlines such as 'Tourists flee Bangkok bloodbath.' I suppose it sells papers.

With the resulting cancellations being the order of the next few weeks, an already precariously balanced tourist industry had been dealt a severe blow, from which it is only now just recovering. The fight between successive governments, yellow shirts and red shirts, and a handful of blues has done nothing to further democracy or the economy of the country.

It's all a shame really. It's a battle nobody wins, though as a spin-off hotels have slashed their rates to try and boost the flagging figures and give their staff something to do, rather than retrench. If you want to visit Thailand, come on over now, it will never be cheaper.

Gik karaoke bar

My wife and I were coming home the other night after a very pleasant evening at a good restaurant, Tim's Place, Chaiyapruek Road, if you want to know. The wife suggested that we stop at a karaoke bar on the way for a laugh. Som knows my feeling about karaoke; this was no high class karaoke she was suggesting, but one of the many suburban karaoke venues.

If you have ever strayed from the main thoroughfares in the major towns, you will have seen one of these. Fairy lights and fair maidens are situated at the front of the establishment, and there is a stage with a fluorescent painted backdrop at the rear. In between is comfortable sofa-style seating in semi-darkness. All have a roof, but many are open-sided and it is obvious that expense is spared.

We parked and came in by the side, rather than running the gauntlet of the aforementioned fair maidens. Since I had come with a woman in tow

I was not accosted, but I was probably the object of conjecture. People must have been wondering why I was there. As they say in the UK, this was a case of carrying coals to Newcastle.

We settled on a vacant sofa and we were asked what we wanted to drink. We ordered a large bottle of beer; small bottles don't feature on the drinks menu of places like this.

On the stage was a young girl with a microphone attempting to sing to the karaoke monitor. I think it would be fair to say that she had not had any voice training, however, for the North-Eastern Isaan music this is probably an advantage. Issan music is probably best described as discords set to percussion.

There was sign writing on the backdrop which my wife translated as the 'Gik' Karaoke Bar. Now a 'gik' in Thai roughly translates to 'lover' or someone you have an affair with. The establishment's *raison d'etre* was becoming apparent.

There were certainly enough young ladies to pick a 'gik' from, around 20 at a rough head count (and there were some rough heads amongst them, believe me. Use-by dates had long expired). However, it wasn't the heads that caught my attention; it was the get-ups. Undoubtedly a collection of the most outlandish costumes you will ever see in one place at one time.

I'll begin with the boots. These were in all colours and most had platform soles of at least eight cm, three inches if you are an old imperial person. They all came to at least mid calf, though most were even higher and came to the knee.

Moving on upwards, the singers all had skirts which were so short, a pelmet would be a better description. They were super-low at the hips and super-short at the hem, barely covering the backside. Teamed with this revealing lower costume were black knickers, which were worn over white knickers and pantyhose. This is another one of those amazing contradictions for which Thailand is famous, 'if my knickers can be seen, then you won't see the underneath ones.' Moving on upwards, there was a skimpy little top which just covered the breasts, if there had not also been a large brassiere worn for visual protection. This bra was generally not the same colour as the top.

The floor show was non-stop, with the singers performing one song and being immediately followed on stage by the next, and the next and the next. There was no introduction of the numbers, no Barbra Streisand, Beyonce, Shakira or local Thai pop diva Tata Young. There was also no applause (that much I did agree with). At one stage an announcement was made which my wife told me was an invitation for the audience to come up and sing. Nobody moved, and I was certainly not going to.

If one of the singers pleased someone in the audience, paper garlands could be purchased for 100 baht, and these were placed around the neck of the singer. Som told me that at the end of the night, the garlands were handed back in to the manageress and the girl would receive about 20 baht per garland. Everything has its price (and its profit).

As my eyes became accustomed to the low lighting levels I looked around to see what my fellow audience members were like. Most looked like middle-aged male office workers, they all had a beer in front of them and all, without exception, were surrounded by three or four 'giks'. It was obvious that the karaoke bar was a place where Thai males could go for company. With the restrictions in Thai culture as far as a little hanky-panky is concerned, this would allow some freedom, in an environment which was (on the outside) respectable enough.

I asked Som if the girls would be available for short-time liaisons, and she reluctantly volunteered, 'I think so,' which, when you strip away the Thai modesty and reluctance to point fingers, means 'definitely so.'

This karaoke bar culture is then something that fits into the Thai community. It is not a beer bar stocked with young ladies of easy virtue (or prostitutes if we are feeling unkind), but a karaoke venue which provides beer, entertainment, company and a bit of rumpy-pumpy if that is what you want.

After half an hour we had finished our large bottle of beer and received the bill for 110 baht (40-50 baht in the supermarket). I also left a 10 baht tip, after all, I had been entertained and educated.

Two wheels and no brakes

Thailand, like many countries in Asia, has almost more motorcycles than people. It has also begun to send its people into the world motorcycling championship sphere, with Ratthapark Wilairot competing in the Moto-GP 250cc class with distinction in his first season. Yet despite the plethora of motorcycles, Thailand has yet to produce a speedway rider. I believe it is probably because of a lack of information or even ambition, rather than a lack of potential talent.

We have all had many ambitions in our lives. How many of us wanted to be firemen and ride in a big red fire truck, when we were small children? Quite a few I would imagine, but it was never my childhood dream—I wanted to be a speedway rider. For those of you who have never heard of it, speedway is a motorcycle sport that involves four and sometimes up to six riders competing over four anti-clockwise laps of an oval circuit. The motorcycles used usually only have one gear and no brakes. The races often take place on flat, uneven surfaces and the competitors use this surface to slide their bikes into the bends. The bikes can reach speeds of up to 110 km/h.

I blame my father for this (which is why we have fathers—to be the recipients of 'blame') as it was he who took me to Meadowbank Speedway in Edinburgh to watch the Saturday night's competition under floodlights when I was a young boy. The sound of the single cylinder speedway bikes, the smell of Castrol R and the shoulder to shoulder racing had me enthralled.

The captain of the local team, Edinburgh Monarchs, was an Australian called Jack Young, who was the world champion at that time. Jack Young was so good, he had to give all the other riders a 50 metre start to give them even a fighting chance. Jack Young was my boyhood hero and I would queue up at the back of the pits to get his autograph. I even became a lifetime member of the Meadowbank Speedway Supporters Club. Not that my life membership has done me much good, since they tore down the speedway to build the arena for the Commonwealth Games of 1970. I think that's called 'progress' or something. But even the demolition of the track did nothing to stop my ambition to be a speedway rider, just like Jack Young.

When I was 17 I was undecided as to whether I should enter medical school or take up speedway racing. My parents made the decision for me and it was books, bones and scalpels. I would make the same decision for my children, so I do not hold a grudge about it.

However, the desire to emulate my boyhood hero remained with me, despite graduating as a doctor. I also went motor racing where I had a fair degree of success. Saturday nights were always speedway nights and I would curse if it ever rained and the meeting was cancelled.

I came to know the speedway racers, the engineers, crew and riders. They all became my patients, as I was probably the only doctor in Australia who understood their love of the sport. I had also competed in Moto-X, where my only distinction was that I had never come last (although I have to admit, it was close at times) I still had never swung my leg over a speedway bike, though the opportunity was getting closer.

I received a call one Saturday morning from the race engineer for one of Australia's top professional riders, John Titman. John had cut the tendons in his left hand in an industrial accident on the Friday and had been operated on. He was in hospital, where he was to stay till the middle of the following week. This was a big problem, John had to ride at the speedway that night, or he would lose his chance to ride in the world championship final. His engineer wanted to know if there was any way I could get John out of the hospital and in a fit state to race.

This was a big ask. My first stop was with the hand surgeon, who was less than impressed, but reluctantly allowed John out of hospital, provided I took full responsibility for the repairs to the tendon. By this stage it was early afternoon and we went to the engineering shop where we designed and fabricated an aluminium 'glove' which stopped him moving his middle, ring and small fingers, but still would let him grip the handlebar. The index finger was left out, but covered with a rubber glove so he could operate the clutch lever at the start of each race.

We arrived at the speedway, where I fitted the glove on John, and his engineer adjusted the clutch lever so that the index finger could release it. As he went out for the first heat, I was crossing my fingers.

After each heat we would have to take the alloy glove off and the rubber for the index finger, clean the hand and then get him ready for the next heat. I don't know how, but we managed it. John rode below his best, naturally, but placed well enough to go through to the next round of the world championship (where he finished sixth at the world final in Europe).

When John Titman returned to Australia he came to see me to thank me for my part in getting him to the championship.

'What do I owe you, Doc?'

My reply took him aback somewhat. 'A ride on your speedway bike!'

And so, 32 years after I imagined it, it happened. A 43-year-old novice swung his leg over a world championship speedway bike at the Ipswich speedway, a 500cc methanol burning bike with no brakes. My boyhood ambition was finally realised. I was never going to set the dirt tracks alight, but I had done it—and before you ask, I didn't fall off.

Believe it or not, a similar situation has arisen in Thailand. A few years ago, a Scandinavian chap brought a speedway bike to Thailand, thinking it would be easy to race against the Thais, and become a hero in his own lunchtime. Unfortunately for him, there were no Thai speedway tracks, no Thai speedway riders, and no Thai speedway bikes. He didn't stay in Thailand for long, and he left his motorcycle behind him.

I have a friend, Colin Marshall, an ex-motorcycle road racer who has lived in Thailand for many years. In fact, he is one of the few *farangs* who has officially become Thai, and he has that same speedway motorcycle in his shed. We often discuss taking it out to one of the dirt fields and firing it up. We talk about the possibility of starting the speedway craze here in Thailand, then we talk about how much money we haven't got, and then we have another beer. In today's troubled financial times, it would be difficult to find a rich backer for this speedway project, especially since it is almost unheard in Thailand.

The speedway motorcycle is still waiting to be fired up, and this 67-year-old is ready to throw his leg over once again. All we need is money. Any offers?

Siamese twins

Siamese twins are always newsworthy, and these days with the advances in surgical techniques, they have a greater chance of independent survival.

The incidence in the world is about one in 400,000 births, though it is difficult to get exact figures. Stillborn Siamese twins have been disposed of and the mothers have remained ignorant of their anatomical problems. Also known as conjoined twins, there was a case in Russia where they were kept in a paediatric institution and the mother told they had died at birth. There is still a lot of superstition surrounding Siamese twins, even in the present day.

But did they really come from Siam (the old name for Thailand)? In a way, yes, though the condition is not restricted to Siam. They can occur in any country, but the most publicised conjoined twins did come from Siam, and gave the condition its original name. They were called Chang and Eng Bunker, born in the Mekong valley to a Chinese father and a Thai-Chinese mother in 1811. Their surname came later after they had lived in America for some time, as in 1811 Siamese people did not have any family name. A law requiring Thai people to have a surname was not enacted until 1913 by King Vajaravudh, Rama VI.

In 1829, Chang and Eng were discovered in old Siam by a British merchant, Robert Hunter, and exhibited as a curiosity around the world. This was the fate of anyone who had some major deformity in those days, and live adult Siamese twins would have been very rare, with most never making it through childhood.

Chang and Eng were joined at the breast-bone (sternum) by a small piece of cartilaginous tissue. Their livers were fused but independently complete. Unfortunately, 19th century medicine did not have the diagnostic imaging equipment necessary or the surgical know-how to separate them. Modern advances in diagnostic and surgical techniques would have allowed them to be easily separated.

Upon termination of their contract with their discoverer, they successfully went into business for themselves, which is really quite amazing, considering their origin in rural Siam. In 1839, while visiting Wilkesboro, North Carolina, the twins were attracted to the town and settled there, eventually becoming naturalized United States citizens.

They had become wealthy, thanks to Robert Hunter and his world tours, so they settled on a plantation, bought slaves, and adopted the name 'Bunker'. They were accepted as respected members of the community. On 13 April 1843, they married two sisters: Chang to Adelaide Yates and Eng to Sarah Anne Yates. Chang and his wife had ten children; Eng and his wife had twelve. The mechanical difficulties in procreation would have been even more of a problem than the mental acceptance of a strange three or four some in those more straight-laced days.

Unfortunately, the sisters squabbled and eventually two separate households were set up just west of Mount Airy, North Carolina—Chang and Eng would alternate, spending three days at each home. During the American Civil War Chang's son Christopher and Eng's son Stephen both fought for the Confederacy.

I read a most interesting book about Chang and Eng, written by author Darin Strauss. It was a fictional account of the lives of the famous Siamese twins in which Strauss tells their story in a flash-back style, alternating chapters between the twin boys early life in Siam and their later, and married, life in America.

He has done an excellent job at imagining just how life must have been like for the twins, joined by a tough 'ligament' making it such that each was dependant upon the other, and in fact, when Chang died, Eng also did the same very shortly afterwards. The epilogue is very poignant. Chang has died in his sleep and 'he (Eng) draws his brother closer to him. Eng takes his twin in his arms. This is the image Sarah keeps of her husband for the rest of her life. Eng dies.'

Where Strauss has done so well is to use the real framework and muse over what life must have been like, not only for them, but for their wives as well. The courtship between the conjoined twins and their wives, Adelaide and Sarah could never have been normal (though there was always one of the twins as a chaperone, I suppose).

Author Darin Strauss does go to some lengths in a disclaimer at the end of the book, stating, 'But the book in your hand hopes to be ruled a novel and not a history. Most of its people and situations result strictly from the imagination. Where I have discarded or finessed or invented the details of Chang and Eng's life, it was only to elbow the facts toward a novel's own idea of truth, which is something else entirely.'

Novel it may be, but it answered several questions in a most logical way. A most interesting book and one you will enjoy if you are interested in the story of the original Siamese twins.

However, as I have already mentioned, this type of twinning did not originate in Siam, and one of the earliest documented cases of conjoined twins is Mary and Eliza Chulkhurst, also known as the Biddenden Maids. Born in 1100, the sisters lived for 34 years in Biddenden, County of Kent, England. Mary and Eliza, though often depicted as joined at the hip and shoulders, were more likely joined at the buttocks and lower backs. After the death of one sister, the 'doctors' of the day hoped to save the life of the other by separating them surgically, however, the surviving twin refused, declaring, 'As we came together, we will go together.' She died several hours later.

Upon their deaths, a local church received 20 acres of land. In remembrance of their generosity, small cakes and biscuits imprinted with the image of the sisters were given to the poor every Easter Sunday. Nearly 900 years after their deaths, the Biddenden Maids were still honoured by this unique service.

Conjoined twins elicit very intense responses, with the ethics in separating them still being discussed. If it is a simple surgical situation, then the conflict is not as great as to when there may be shared organs, making it such that one twin would have to be sacrificed for the other, but if an operation is not done, both will die. Herein lies a moral dilemma.

I have personal experience of one pair of Siamese twins in Pattaya. These two girls had been separated, having been joined at the lower part of their bodies. Unfortunately, the parents did not have any money and although the operation had apparently been done for free, they were unable, or even perhaps unwilling, to continue follow up surgical care. I managed to find a *farang* sponsor and the two girls did get some further treatment, but then disappeared as quickly as they had come into view. They would be around 10 years of age today, if they have survived.

By the way, Chang and Eng continue to be of interest with a documentary having been made of their lives in 2009, called *The Siamese Connection*. Both Chang and Eng's great-granddaughters were interviewed about their famous Siamese (Thai) forebears for the making of the documentary.

Will we all survive?

We are living in an age of doom, gloom and despair. Due to some financial crisis, which I don't pretend to really understand but know it has something to do with US money lenders overstretching themselves and subprime mortgages, the whole house of cards has come crashing down. That includes your house of cards and mine—no matter where we are.

Mind you, I would have to doubt any lender with the name of Fannie Mae or Freddie Mac. Just what sort of names are those for rock solid financial institutions? I suggest you start up a money lending called Fanny Adams or Suzi Wong. They're just as credible.

I do wonder about the US sometimes. I read today that voters in Riviera Beach in Florida passed a law banning low slung trousers that show your underwear. Not only did they pass the law, but a local defender of the law arrested a 17-year-old cyclist because he could see four or five inches of blue and black boxer shorts.

This could be serious for the young fellow as the fine for a first offence of saggy baggies is $150. Habitual offenders get jail terms. I would imagine that after the third time, it will be castration. I ask you, with all the problems inherent in the US economy, is this really the best that the Riviera Beach residents can do?

Some blame has to be laid at the door of oil cartels for the present financial climate. Overnight, oil suddenly went from around $30 dollars a barrel to almost $150. Questions have to be asked as to why this happened. The costs to get the stuff out of the ground did not triple. The latest news is that OPEC has decided to slow down oil production to keep the price of crude as high as possible. So are we being held over the proverbial barrel (we are!) while the sandy deserts are being transformed into luxury hotels and golf courses using the increased profits from the pumps?

Since the world depends on goods being shipped country to country, the increased transportation costs have been passed on to the consumers and everything has gone up in price, even my son's nappies. If he would only grow up quicker so that he wouldn't pee the bed, I would happily throw them back at the manufacturer, or even better—at OPEC. Used, of course.

In a magnanimous gesture, the airlines then told us that they would not increase fares. What they didn't say was that they would add a fuel surcharge instead, thus doubling the total price. Incidentally, beware of advertised fares on the internet. I was looking to see how much it would cost to fly to the UK to visit my mother. 28,000 baht return (about $800) was advertised. This was great news; I was ready to buy two. However, when I enquired further there was a small matter of fuel surcharge and tax, which brought it up to 45,000 baht (about $1,285).

Consequently the number of people flying away on holidays has fallen. The Tourism Authority of Thailand says the numbers are down 30%. I wager that it is more like 50%; if the truth be known (When has anyone believed governments anywhere?) With the Thai economy's reliance on international tourism, the current situation is not good. The results of all this are half-empty hotels and even emptier restaurants. Real estate agents have nobody to sell the new built houses to. This is a recipe for more doom and disaster.

One of my friends is a hotelier in Thailand and in October 2008 published the following projection for Thai business over the next few months.

He was not optimistic, saying,

'I believe for Thailand's Tourism industry and I guess pretty much everywhere else in the world, what is happening in the USA's banking sector will have many implications for travel and tourism. I think it is going to be a roller coaster time ahead and the outcome may not be something to look forward to.

'The squeeze on credit between banks and the demise of the weakest will have a knock-on effect into other areas. Even if the USA passes the emergency bill and injects hundred's of billions of dollars into the system is it enough and is it in time? Frankly, as a consumer I feel reluctant to spend money at this time, not quite knowing what is around the corner. Discretionary spend is being cut to a minimum in case I need to dip into reserves and savings. I believe I am not alone in this thinking, which multiplied many times over will impact many industries including tourism.

'With banking under pressure, real estate sales will be squeezed and buyers more difficult to find. This impacts the sale of building materials and ultimately home appliances. The sale of new cars, electronic products and holidays will also likely diminish. Follow this through to conferences, meetings and accommodation linked to product launches, exhibitions and sales seminars, they are likely to be affected negatively too.

'(Hotel) Occupancies below 50 percent are becoming the norm in Bangkok and pressure to reduce costs increases with decreasing occupancy.

'Let's hope that the banking sector can resolve their challenges quickly and then we can start to look forward to happier times.'

In a personal memo to me, he said, 'In Sept 2008 I had to let go 88 part-time staff from my compliment of 600. I guess they will not be taking holidays this year.'

Yes, the American sub-prime fallout is affecting Thailand too.

So, will we survive the current turmoil in Thailand? Will the tourists return? Will the world's financial markets ruin us? Ask anyone and they all have long faces. As I write this, we've just gone through the low season. Will we even have a high season this year?

Quite honestly, what we are going through is nothing new. Thailand has had its history of political upheavals and coups. Thailand has had bloodshed on the streets and in the universities. Thailand has weathered reports of visitors 'fleeing Bangkok' and nervous nations issuing travel warnings. When you think about it, how have we *farangs* survived in this country?

One of the reasons we have survived, and will survive the present downturn comes from the very nature of the Thai people themselves. Have you ever met a friendlier race of people? Where else in the world can you go and be greeted with such smiles?

Sure, we have prices that are lower than many other tourist destinations, but tourists do not chose Thailand just for its bargains. In my view, the 'Amazing Thailand Grand Sales' promotion, so beloved by the Tourism Authority, does not bring tourists to this country.

No, cheap items do not bring back the tourists in large numbers. The Thai people can with their friendly nature, and we too can help in the reconstruction of the high season.

How many of you have invited your friends and relatives overseas to come and visit? Rather than re-plying to anxious emails to say that you are OK, have you said that 'everything' is OK and they can ignore the pushed panic buttons by overseas embassies. How many of you have offered to find good cheap accommodation for your friends (and there are certainly bargains to be had)?

Rather than waiting for the tourists to come back while staring apathetically at the wall, we can actively attract tourism by pointing out that Thailand was, and still is, an exciting and colourful country where the tourist dollar still goes a long way; the climate was, and still is, superb. The infrastructure is one of the best in Southeast Asia; the golf courses are still green and the caddies are still smiling; real estate bargains are waiting for them. Hospitals are still second to none and the prices for medical procedures are still around half of that charged in the West.

We live here and enjoy the living 12 months a year, every year. Get the people from your home countries to come and sample it with you. If we all bring out one tourist each, we will have done something to restore prosperity. Think about it.

Another Valentino Rossi?

If you have even the slightest interest in motorcycling, you could not have missed the fact that Italian Valentino Rossi has become the rider with the most wins in history, beating the mark set by another Italian racing legend, Giacomo Agostini.

If you live in Thailand, or have even visited here for more than 24 hours, it is impossible to miss the fact that two wheels reign supreme in this country. Every street has rows of parked motorcycles, so close together you wonder just how the rider(s) managed to dismount. (In fact, the secret is they park across the tails of the parked motorcycles to dismount, wade in and shift the parked motorcycles even closer together and slide their one in between.)

With such a culture of two wheeling, it is then surprising that there have not been too many Thais to compete on two wheels overseas. Currently there is only one that I know of, Ratthapark Wilairot, who competed in 2008 in the Moto GP 250 class. Ratthapark competed in the Japanese GP as a wild card in 2007 and did well to finish 10th. He was the runner-up in the Japanese national championships last year, and is also the first Thai rider to compete in a full season of the 250cc class of the FIM World Motorcycle Championships, riding for the Thai-Honda PTT-SAG team.

There may be more, but if so, they are certainly not household names. For that matter, Prince Bira is an unknown amongst the ordinary Thais. This is a shame, as Prince Bira was the first international Thai (in those days Siam) sportsman to compete at the top level of international motor sport. His world ranking being significantly higher than Thailand's current crop of tennis players for example.

So how do we get some young Thai motorcycling hero up there? Just as the current Formula One drivers go through a well documented ladder to climb from Go-Karts through to the top echelon (for example just look at the current hot property Lewis Hamilton who started at age eight) then you will find the two wheeled heroes do the same. Valentino Rossi actually began in kart racing aged five, because his mother thought it less dangerous having him on four wheels (incidentally, she is correct), but despite that, by the time he was 10 he was on two wheels racing Minimoto.

There is a light at the end of the tunnel for Thai racers who are regularly arrested for racing on Bangkok's expressways late at night. And it is not just a few, the police literally arrest over 100 'illegal' racers, so the interest is there. I recently attended a motorcycle racing meeting at the Bira International Circuit in Thailand, promoted by Grand Prix International (GPI), and I was immediately taken by the different classes racing that weekend. Everything from small step-throughs to 1000cc big bikes. The riders also covered everyone from ultra-competitive eight year old Thais to semi-retired Americans racing 600's for fun.

This was also a very special meeting, according to Anothai Eamlumnow from Grand Prix International, as it has been 20 years since they last promoted motorcycle racing. To mark the event, and its importance, the President of GPI Dr. Prachin Eamlumnow and the newly elected mayor of Pattaya Itthipol Khunplome, were in attendance at the grand opening on the Sunday.

Two Thai riders stood out from the meeting as future champions. Kemin Kubo was eight years old and Kiettisak Chuaywiset was nine. Both were riding Honda Click Super Star step-throughs and both were very, very small. So small in fact that when lined up stationary on the grid before the race started, they could not remain seated on the saddle, but had to slip off and literally stand on one leg beside the motorcycle. When the starting lights went out, they had to push their step-throughs forward and jump on to the saddles. And what is more, both of the boys rode like champions, hanging off the side of the bike like Valentino Rossi would do, with Kemin coming through the pack to win.

So if we have child prodigies on two wheels, why do we only have one rider competing overseas at the top levels, while the Japanese have many riders in the top groups? The simple answer is money.

In today's commercial world, any rider needs big bucks behind him to even get one foot on the ladder of international success. Compared to four wheel motorsports, the two wheel novices do get it easier financially on the way to the top. By the way, I am not saying that top level Moto GP is cheap, but it is small change compared to the route to the top of Formula One.

In the Moto GP 250cc class, the cost of running a current 250cc team is still huge: something like $1.6 million to lease an Aprilia 250cc bike for the season and at the end of the season you have to hand it back. However, the 250cc class is one rung from the top, whilst with four wheels you are looking at around $4 million to be one rung from Formula One. You can see why the frustrated taxi motorcycle rider on your local street corner is restricted to racing on the expressways at midnight.

It will need the government to get behind Thai youth, but with the current political bickering, it is unlikely much will happen to promote young Thais internationally. That is why I say 'Well done GPI, and well done Kemin Kubo and Kiettisak Chuaywiset Honda Click Super Stars!'

By the time young Evan, who is currently motorcycle mad, gets to eight years of age, there may even be a well defined road to the top. Stranger things have happened. After all, we managed to get rid of a hugely unpopular Thai prime minister because he cooked up some dishes in a TV cooking show.

A touch of magic

I opened the newspaper the other day and there was a house advert saying, 'Surprise Surprise! Expect the unexpected,' in their Classified section. I glanced across at the next page and there was an advert from a hotel wanting staff. One staff member they required was (and I quote exactly from their large advert) 'Hostess required—male.' Yes indeed, that was fairly unexpected. Perhaps they were hoping for a ladyboy, or perhaps it was just another quirk of miscommunication?

In actual fact, living in Thailand is rather like that —you can always expect the unexpected any day of the week. You never quite know what you are going to see, read, feel or smell next. For me, every day has a touch of magic in it somewhere. I have mentioned elsewhere the wonderful chap with the gold sequined outfit and the bicycle. Not quite the norm, and very much unexpected.

It is probably difficult for readers in the West to imagine themselves in my shoes. Why do I describe living here as a touch of magic? Let me attempt to explain. The first magical thing happens on driving to work each morning. There's no road rage. There may be traffic jams, there may be motorcyclists risking life and limb, but there is no aggression.

There are also many Mums and Dads taking their children to school, not in the soft-roader four wheel drive, air-conditioned, automatic, people mover beloved by the American hockey Moms, but in or on transport that would be banned by western lawmakers.

I will see battered old motorcycles with rickety sidecar made from steel rod left over from a building site, with three kids sitting in the chair and another couple hanging on to Mum like koala bears. For even the lowest paid workers, children's education is a family priority. These children come from families that cannot afford people movers, but every last one of them, on the noisy contraption, are outfitted in spotless uniforms and they all have big smiles. Some will wave to me as I drive past. The day's first magic moment.

In my workplace, there is respect given to this old *farang*, given by way of *wai*'s, smiles, bobbing of the head or other gestures. I can even get a salute from an 'admiral', as I talked about earlier.

Some afternoons I go to what I call my 'city office' which is opposite the Royal Garden Plaza shopping centre. I will generally have lunch at one of the outlets, where my order is taken by a smiling young cutie which makes me feel young again, as well as hungry. The smile is returned by me. She has helped lighten my day. Magic, surely.

While sitting waiting for lunch, I have the opportunity to eavesdrop, and the true 'internationality' of my life in Thailand really hits home. I am surrounded by Germans, Italians, Russians, Americans, Chinese, Koreans and even Scots, Irish and English. This reminds me that I am just one little speck in the global village and Thailand is the magic dust to allow all these differing races to coexist. Incidentally, in my little Jomtien village, the men in the houses on either side and across the street are Thai, Swiss, German and Dutch, all married to Thai women. So perhaps Thai women are that magic dust?

On the way back through the mall, I will pass several gorgeous girls, some office workers, some university students and some, dare I say it—sex workers. I am not accosted, but I am certainly given a big smile by all of them. Eyes are locked for a second, a visual promise awaits, but we all pass each other by, the proverbial ships in the night.

But now I have another smile too. Life is not passing me by; a life experience is possibly there for the taking if I were to pursue it. I don't have to, or want to, but the experience makes me walk taller and makes me more aware of myself, and perhaps even a little (probably undeserved) proud of myself. Am I still attractive? Perhaps I am. Perhaps there is a touch of Thai magic in the air that strips 40 years from my appearance. It's better than plastic surgery and there's no pain or cost involved.

Later in the afternoon I may receive a phone call from my daughter. She misses me. When will I come home? Soon, I tell her. I stop off on the way to buy some sweets for her and her brother to share when I get home. When I get out of the car at the local 7-11 shop (there is one on every corner and two in between) I go past small food carts making satays or grilling chickens, with billowing smoke and wonderful aromas. Something that you don't see, or are not allowed in the West. These are also for me, little magic moments.

Being a second time Dad who can bask in the love of his little family and give them some of my time (as well as the ordered sweeties), instead of striving and slaving night and day in the office to meet the mortgage and pay the credit cards. In doing that, in the West we voluntarily extinguish some of our life's magic moments. Thailand has given me the opportunity to savour them.

I have, however, omitted one of what I consider to be the best sights in all of Thailand. It has to be when I spot large, amorphous grey elephants lumbering majestically down the road, trunks and tails swinging in unison, a *mahout* perched on its neck tugging its ears for changes of direction. The first time I experienced this was on one of my holiday trips to Thailand before I moved here permanently. Stopping to feed the elephant was the high point of my vacation that year. There are those who would condemn the idea of elephants carrying food on their backs for the tourists to buy and then feed back to the elephant, but I do not. We humans have taken away their forests where they used to roam. We have mechanical devices to haul the teak logs from the (few remaining) forests, and there is a limit to the number of elephants in touristy elephant corrals. Forget the so-called morality, by buying the elephant a snack I am helping both it and its *mahout* to survive. And for me it is another magic moment as I stroke its rough skinned trunk and look into those wonderful large brown eyes. Sometimes the children have to wait another 15 minutes before Dad comes home with sweeties in his pocket.

News today—chip wrappers tomorrow

The world's media is a fairly cynical bunch. Catchphrases such as 'Never let the truth stand in the way of a good story' do not come out of thin air, but have some basis in their approaches. There are many good reasons for it, let me assure you, and I know some of them first-hand. (The camera toting photojournalists also came up with the camera exposure setting for all news items described as 'f8 and be there'. Why 'be there'? Because many war correspondents have covered the action from the safety of their hotel rooms. In neighbouring countries!)

At the time of writing this, Thailand and especially Bangkok has been very prominent in international news because of the takeover of the airports by the People's Alliance for Democracy, known as the PAD or yellow shirts. With all the fervour that is normally reserved for fighting in Basra, an enthusiastic journalist filed the following item.

'Flights into Thailand have been thrown into chaos Wednesday after explosions at two Bangkok airports wounded four people and triggered the closure of its main international gateway—a major hub in the region for travelers, authorities said.'

The emotive use of 'explosions' and 'wounded' are designed to produce 'shock, horror' reactions and this item could well have been followed up by 'Terrified tourists flee the Thai capital,' as was used before by reporters when the military coup of 2006 took place. That was when the 'terrified tourists' were enjoying the opportunity to be photographed with a tank on the main streets in Bangkok. It should also be pointed out that the local Thais were wrapping yellow ribbons around the gun barrels and bringing cold drinks and food to the Army tank drivers.

But let's return to the 'triggered the closure' item. The airports were closed because the PAD walked in and took them over. This bears no resemblance to the events in Munich. Just like the 2006 coup, it all just happened, as the thousands of PAD supporters walked in and occupied the terminals.

'How did Thai protesters manage it?' asked Jonathan Head of the BBC News, in Bangkok. 'How could a country as advanced and as dependent on exports and tourism as Thailand allow such a vital transport hub to be stormed by a mob that never numbered more than a few thousand?'

The answer was really quite simple. The police had done such an inept job of chasing away the PAD during its sit-in at Government House, by haphazardly firing tear gas canisters into the crowd, that they were reluctant to act again. In fact, the chief of police, who voiced the 'do nothing' order, was dismissed and demoted by the government after this and a new top man was installed. That did nothing either, as the police on the ground did not want a brawl either. Brawling is not really the 'Thai way,' in circumstances such as this.

As a race, Thais are still predominantly a non-violent people, despite what you might hear or read in the popular media. Isolated instances do not make it widespread.

By this stage of the impasse, the government played its last card. They asked the army to intervene. It wouldn't, mainly because the majority of the army supported the cause of the PAD, even if not the PAD itself.

So the protestors in their yellow shirts unrolled their mats, ate their meals, listened to the PAD leaders while waving their plastic hand-clappers in agreement and were entertained by the never-ending stream of bands, singers and musicians who had come to support their cause as well.

Those who could not attend in person watched it all on TV, as the PAD even had its own TV station. This was no army of AK 47 waving zealots and terrorists, looting the duty-free areas of the terminals. This was an army of middle aged ladies with poodles, united in their desire to see true democracy in Thailand. (However, it would probably be the first time, if they were successful.)

That the incumbent government was corrupt was further borne out by the Constitution Court finding most of the ruling coalition parties in the government had indulged in vote-buying at the grass roots level, so their vaunted grass roots 'majority' was certainly in doubt. Their parties were disbanded, and their executives barred from politics for five years. Showing a tacit acceptance of their guilt, the major party (called the PPP, which was in itself a reformation of convicted ex-PM Thaksin Shinawatra's TRT party) had already formed a new party before the Constitution Court verdict was given.

Along with the government ouster verdict, the PAD then withdrew from Suvarnabhumi Airport (pronounced 'Soowannapoom', by the way), and air travel returned to normal by that weekend. The terminals were just as they had been left when the PAD had walked in one week earlier. Of course there were mutterings by the opposing red shirt (pro government supporters) that weapons had been found, plus bullets and bombs. Strange that the PAD should have taken the ordnance into the airport, never used it, and then left it all behind. How forgetful of them. No abandoned poodles were found, however. I leave you to make up your own mind.

There were many travellers who were disadvantaged by the closure of the airports, but the tourists I met were all disappointed when they were told they were now going home. They wanted to stay on, especially when the hotels were offering really budget rates to make life easier for them. 'Bugger it,' said Alan from London. 'I thought I was going to get an extra week on my holidays.'

No, despite what you have read, protests in Thailand are quite different from those you have seen in Bosnia, Iraq or Afghanistan. Protests here are localised to a small area where you take your plastic hand-clapper and listen to the speeches and sing along with the entertainers. If you were not in the area, you would not even know that it was going on.

During the last three months, I did not see one ex-Army WWII surplus helmet. It was never needed, not even in Bangkok. The noodle shop on the corner of my street continued to make breakfasts for the school children, as did noodle shop ladies throughout the country, but she did have a yellow ribbon displayed, and I did find a hand-clapper in the doctor's common room.

As Thailand returned to normal, the rest of the world did its bit to hog the media centre stage, with the terrorist attacks in Mumbai, killing close to 200 people, grabbing the headlines. For Thailand, the humdrum happenings of the next day followed that other great newspaper dictum, 'News today, chip wrappers tomorrow!'

Base jumping without
a parachute

Most of the world's knowledge on Paraquat poisoning comes from Western Samoa. Now I'll bet you didn't know that. In Western Samoa, people cannot live with an extreme loss of face, and so it is expected that the person afflicted will commit suicide. Western Samoa does not have any train lines to lie upon or any high buildings worth jumping from, so the unfortunate person is left with walking out to sea and drowning, or swallowing Paraquat, a pesticide.

Let me assure you that if you are in that situation, walk out to sea. Paraquat poisoning is a horrible and slow way to end it all. It takes two weeks while your lungs shrivel irreversibly and you die. There is no turning back during those 14 days. Do not drink Paraquat.

However, it seems that Pattaya has become the base jumping capital of the world. Base, by the way, stands for Building, Antenna, Span, and Earth, whereby the participant jumps off a building, spire, bridge or mountain, wearing only one parachute. However, in Pattaya, they are all done without a parachute.

Once again, it is a cultural thing. There are limited opportunities in Pattaya for people who wish to end it all, much like in Western Samoa. There is a train line, but trains only run once a day, so there's a long wait between the decision being made and the act itself. The waters of Pattaya Bay are so congested, somebody would fish the aspiring suicide out of the water before that final gurgle. That leaves jumping off high buildings, of which Pattaya has plenty.

Unfortunately, ending it all in this way has become something of an epidemic. The *Pattaya Mail* reports that around one or two *farangs* a week take their lives in this fashion. It's such a shame.

I will tell you of one such suicide. *Jim* was a British chap I knew quite well, or so I thought. He had told everyone that he was a British company owner, with a large real estate holding still in London. He was living off the rentals and didn't need to work. He also had a very large sum in his London bank on fixed deposit. I suppose we envied him in a way. He had put in the hard work and could now sit back and enjoy the fruit of his labours. Because he was financially sound, I put him in contact with a friend of mine who had a condominium to rent and he signed the contract for a room on the 16th floor.

Jim was a good photographer and had some expensive camera gear and enjoyed taking photos of the ladies in Pattaya, there was always a ready pool of subjects. Some of these shots were so good he began to get paid work from some of the establishments, so he was usually found hanging around the bars at night.

We did note that *Jim* was not a generous chap, despite his good income. In fact he knew every cut-price deal in all of the bars, but when we went out with him, we would always end up with the tab. He was also not someone who dressed flashily or expensively. *Jim* was a shorts and flip-flops man, but then again, so are many others in Pattaya.

Then one day he announced that he was not going to take any more photographs as he was tired of being used. He was so resolute over this that he sold his camera and gave away any remaining bits and pieces. We all thought that this would be a passing phase, and we would soon see him back at the bars with his wide grin and camera at the ready.

The next we heard was from his landlord who said that *Jim* seemed to be depressed recently, so he had been taking him out to dinner and for a few drinks at *Jim*'s favourite bars.

That weekend, *Jim* jumped from the balcony of his rented condominium. From that height, death would have been instantaneous.

In the wash-up of it all, it turned out that *Jim* had no real estate holdings in London. He had no income from rentals. He was not a company owner. And on top of that, he was months behind in his rent.

We began to piece this human tragedy together. He had obviously sold his camera to get enough to live on.

The reason he went to all the beer bars with balloons outside was because this indicated free food. He had built up such a framework of lies that he could not retreat without blowing his own fabricated past. He had run himself down a one-way alley, from which he felt there was no way out.

We all felt a little guilty after that, but none of us had been in possession of the full facts. The reason he never picked up the tab was that he never had the money to pay for it. We all just thought he was somewhat stingy. I did not know he was behind in his rent. His landlord did not know he had sold his camera and nobody knew the real story of his past. It is only with hindsight that you get 20/20 vision.

Of course, if he had come clean and admitted his situation, we could all have helped him. We could have put him in the direction of paid employment. His landlord would have declared a moratorium on the rent. He could have got through a very difficult period in his life, a difficult period which he had undoubtedly brought upon himself, but it was not insurmountable.

I was approached a few weeks ago by a chap who said he wanted to thank me. I was somewhat taken aback, because I did not think I had ever met him. He went on to explain that he had been feeling down, but one of the stories in my first book, 'Farang, Thailand through the eyes of an ex-pat' had struck a chord with him and he too had managed to rise above his perceived problems. I must say I was rather chuffed at that. When something you have done helps another human being, it is a good feeling.

And that is the reason why I have included the story on *Jim*. Perhaps another '*Jim*' might read it. Perhaps his friends may recognise the symptoms and avert a disaster. I can only hope so.

By the way, *Jim* was not his real name and many other details have been deliberately altered. Even after death he deserves a little privacy, but the story is true.

Eat your way to good health?

What we eat is something that has fascinated us for centuries. We have made rituals and even fetishes out of eating and drinking, and the oldest gourmet group in the world, the *Chaine des Rotisseurs*, began in 1248 AD and is still going. That's a long lunch.

These days, with our tentative forays into 'real' science, our dietary habits have also been scrutinised and many claims have been made for modifying the kinds of food we eat and what we drink. This in turn has produced legions of people who swear by various food items that can cure everything from falling hair to falling arches (or even the falling stock markets).

Thailand has many of these wonder veggies and herbs. Thai authorities (such as the Thailand Institute of Scientific and Technological Research) claim that many herbs and spices used in everyday Thai cuisine have specific beneficial medicinal properties. Here are just a few of them, and anyone who eats Thai food will recognise them.

Chilli comes in many different species. Almost all Thai food includes chillies somewhere and they all contain capsaicin, a biologically active ingredient claimed to be beneficial to the respiratory system, blood pressure and heart. It is also supposedly an anti-flatulent. My experience has been more of the 'ring of fire' situation the next morning, but that is a personal observation, rather than a scientific conclusion.

Another ubiquitous ingredient is garlic. Dried mature bulbs are used as a flavouring and condiment in Thai cuisine and this is claimed to be an antimicrobial, expectorant and cholesterol lowering agent. The next one I like, just for its name, is Hoary Basil, an annual herbaceous plant with slightly hairy and pale green leaves, eaten either raw or used as a flavouring. It has nothing to do with the bar scene and should not be confused with Holy Basil, and its therapeutic benefits are that it is claimed to be a cough suppressant.

'*Prik Thai*' (pepper) is a branching, perennial climbing plant. The fruiting spikes of the plant are the source of both white and black pepper. It is used as a spice and condiment, and every sidewalk cook has bottles of it as it is sprinkled heavily over everything. Pepper is supposed to bring your temperature down, but it works the other way for me. It will, however, make you sneeze.

Of course, it is very difficult to prove taking Outer Mongolian ground nut leaves or similar items will keep 'something' (usually cancer) at bay, though I do believe it keeps giraffes off the front lawn. Even more outrageous are the claims that some herb, poppy or whatnot can actually 'cure' cancers. Is it all just poppycock?

To be able to prove these claims medical science needs to look at a large group, or population, and compare the cancer experience with another similar large group or population. Ideally, the two groups are matched for age / sex / ethnicity / working environment, location etc. You get no worthwhile results comparing Welsh coal miners with urban Africans, for example. Or even Northeastern Thais with Southern Thais for that matter.

However, a lot of work in these areas is being carried out worldwide. Recently, some results of a fifteen plus year study in Australia were presented at the Prospects for Cancer Prevention Symposium. The findings emerged from the Cancer Council's Melbourne Collaborative Cohort Study, an ongoing research project involving 42,000 Australians who have been monitored since 1990.

Looking at the dietary habits and the cancer connection, Dr Peter Clifton, director of the CSIRO's Nutrition Clinic, said there was 'zero evidence' that eating fruit and vegetables could protect against cancer. The nutritionists and the healthy eating proponents were shattered, leaving them feeling that perhaps now is the time to sell their shares in the Echinacea farm. However, Dr. Clifton's zero evidence result is to me a much more compelling argument than something that comes from folklore, or the lady next door who swears by it. Or the old crone who makes noodle dishes at the corner of our street. What the survey did show was that the three prime risk factors as far as predicting cancers were concerned were identified as obesity, drinking too much alcohol and smoking. Somehow they seem to have missed chilli, garlic and Hoary Basil.

More than that, staying within a healthy body weight range was found to be more important than following particular nutritional guidelines. This means a thin person who does not eat enough fruit and vegetables would have a lower risk of developing cancer than someone who is overweight but eats the recommended daily amount of fruit and five colours of vegetables.

Professor Dallas English, of the Cancer Council of Victoria, told the symposium that despite decades of research, there was no convincing evidence on how modifying one's diet would reduce the risk of cancer.

'The most important thing about diet is limiting energy (kilojoule) intake so people don't become overweight or obese, because this has emerged as a risk factor for a number of cancers, including breast, prostate, bowel and endometrial (uterus),' he said.

Again, despite the aforementioned chilli, garlic and Hoary Basil, I have noticed an increase in the bodily shape of the native Thai population, especially the women. The chrome pole huggers who used to sport two fried eggs chest-wise have now developed real breasts (though there are many silicone varieties available for a price, and much deliberation is done by the overweight beer drinking audience as to the truth of the matter). The adoption of some western eating habits has certainly had an effect.

Let's get back to the food and health situation. According to Professor English, the link between eating red meat and bowel cancer was 'weak' and the Cancer Council supported guidelines advising people to eat red meat three or four times a week. The cattle lobby is still strong it seems.

However, the biggest killer for *farang* males is still heart disease, and it has been shown enough times that healthy eating will lower your chances of having a coronary conclusion, even if it does not protect you against cancer.

Both Professor English and Dr. Clifton predict an increase in the incidence of cancer as a result of the world-wide obesity epidemic, but say exercise can play a vital role in cutting cancer rates, potentially halving the risk of some cancers. That I find a rather sweeping claim, but there is no doubt in my mind that moderate exercise is good for you. Remember the Buddhist adage of following the 'middle way'.

So there you are—get down to a healthy weight and exercise regularly, drink alcohol in moderation only (*farangs* in general do not know what 'moderation' means, though it usually means drinking less than your doctor) and stop smoking. In this way you will lower your chances of both heart disease and cancer.

Goodness me, you might even outlive your doctor!

Motor shows in Thailand

Bangkok is in the strange position of having two motor shows every year. One is the 'official' one at the end of March, given credence by the international accrediting authority called the OICA (Organization Internationale des Constructeurs d'Automobiles). The other is run in November, but without official international sanction.

These motor shows are important in Thai society, and your position in society is linked to the car you drive. Anything with the three-pointed star on it means you have 'arrived'. Since I drive a 10-year-old Daihatsu Mira, this will mean I have 'left' as far as being Hi-So (high society) is concerned.

However, I am fortunate in my capacity as a motoring scribe, in that I get an invitation to the official one each year, and I must say I do enjoy it. If you are interested in cars, here were my thoughts on the 2008 show, and overseas show-goers can compare this with their local one in Birmingham or London or wherever.

(If you are not interested in cars, it might be best to skip this chapter!)

Unfortunately, the 29th running of the Bangkok International Motor Show was not one for people wanting to touch a real exotic. There were no factory exhibits from Porsche, Ferrari, Aston Martin, Maserati, Maybach, Bentley or Rolls-Royce. The mainstays of upmarket motoring were well-represented by Mercedes-Benz, BMW, Lexus and Citroen, though for most of these manufacturers, it was the mid-range that attracted most attention. There was also a stand from the unheard of Mitsuoka (unless you have lived in Japan), but more of that later.

There was no getting away from the fact that the average attendee at the show was more interested in the lower end of the market. The Indian invasion, spearheaded by Tata, the maker of the world's cheapest car, the Nano (THB 87,000 is approximately €1,810), presented their one tonne pick-up, the Xenon. At under THB 600,000 (approximately €12,500), this represented affordable motoring for those with dry rice-fields, wishing to transport a sick buffalo and an extended family of 17 (including grandmother and several babies). The base model Xenon was even going out the door at THB 519,000 during the show (and you could probably throw in a suit and free shirt and a tie in 24 hours at that money).

So the Indians have arrived, but so have the Chinese into Thailand, though rather well disguised as Malaysians at the show. The Naza Forza, styled by

Pininfarina, made its debut and at THB 349,000 (approximately €7,250) for a five door was making great waves. Coming from the Malaysian Naza group, it is sold in Malaysia as the Naza Sutera, but in reality this is the Hafei Lobo from China which is then assembled in Malaysia. In some strange deal, Naza have the rights to manufacture for RHD countries, leaving America and Europe for the Chinese. The Thai distributors were even offering finance over 72 months at THB 4,453 per month. That's about the equivalent of your kid's bus money.

At the other end, let's start with Mercedes-Benz, a manufacturer who has managed to maintain the image of 'quality', despite some disastrous times a few years back. A Benz probably says you have solidly 'arrived', whilst the exotics are generally construed as being owned by the 'nouveau riche'. Yet you can get yourself into a Mercedes-Benz with the new C200 Kompressor at THB 2.999 million or finance at THB 31,600 (approximately €661) per month. With excellent air-conditioning and lovely leather seats you will remain cool and look good, while sitting in the commuter traffic jam.

Of course there were more expensive examples of the Tri-Star, with the lovely little sporty SLK 200 Kompressor allowing you to get the wind gently through the undetectable hair-piece for THB 4.5 million. With deeper pockets you can sit yourself in the 300 SL V6 for THB 7.599 million, or the SL 350 at THB 11.9 million, or go the whole hog in the CL 500 V8 for THB 15.5

million, but that figure does not include the mandatory chauffeur's wages.

Just across the walkway at BITEC was BMW, still (currently) persisting with the infamous Bangle bottom, the unloved rear end styling from Chris Bangle, though the spies say that the next generation will have toned the bustle right down.

BMW have money on every horse in the race this year with the 320d (diesel) getting excellent reviews worldwide from the green movement and at THB 2.85 million a relatively cheap introduction to the fuel miser world of diesel injection.

Variety is the spice of life over there in Munich and there were nine variants in the 3 Series running from THB 2.3 million up to 7.5 million for the 335 coupe and the green movement be damned. But there's more! The M3 coupe at THB 9.9 million with 420 horsepower has enough for anyone. This is performance, but you'll pay for it at the pumps.

With the 5 Series, 6 Series, 7 Series, X Series, M Series and Z Series, BMW provides you with a veritable alphabet and you'll need to dig deep for the 760Li at THB 18.2 million. Very deep.

Lexus was relying on you getting excited at hybrid technology, now extending to their SUV range and the LS luxury limousine, but I frankly think Lexus is somehow missing the boat—and with some prices over THB 10 million, now becoming too expensive.

Citroen had the C6 sedan. A wonderfully Gallic exercise with lines reminiscent of the old CX series and at THB 5.6 million probably a bargain—if you have a servicing agent next door.

Finally, I did promise you the Mitsuoka, Japanese copies of Bentley sedans, without the class or the heritage. Based on Nissan sedans, these ghastly creations ranged in price between THB 3.85 to 5.85 million, but they also had a two door open sports called the Orochi (I believe this is Japanese for 'I am about to vomit') for a staggering THB 11.7 million. You would do better with 33 Naza Forzas for that money. Believe me.

In Thailand, the motor car still reigns supreme, and 1.6 million visitors went to the International Motor Show over the 10 days. All I have to do now is work out how to afford a Benz.

Good karma

I walked to work this morning. Well, that's a slight exaggeration, but I did walk from home to the main (Sukhumvit) road. This is exactly one kilometre and took precisely 12 minutes. Still being able to do sums in my head, I worked out that was five kilometres per hour and hearkening back to the Pattaya Marathon the previous weekend, I could have entered and it would only have taken me eight hours to complete it. Mind you, since the runners were doing it in half the time, I'm glad I didn't enter.

So what brought on such displays of physical prowess? Unfortunately, it was the result of further mechanical unreliability in the mighty Daihatsu Mira— my much unloved and uncared for mode of transport.

In my first book, it was a cylinder head problem that caused me some trouble, but this was different. The evening before, on my way home, I noticed the temperature gauge creeping up. I thought back to when I last checked the water and having come up with the numbers 2-0-0-7 and this being July 2-0-0-8, thought this oversight might have been the cause. On getting home I let it cool down then filled it to the brim, plus the overflow tank. Problem solved, or so I thought.

The next morning, I was no further than two kilometres from home when the rather rapid ascent of the temperature gauge needle rang alarm bells. The last water fill had lasted at least six months. How come this one only lasted six minutes?

I glided to a halt at the side of Sukhumvit Road and opened the bonnet. There was a lot of steam hissing from the radiator. Being somewhat savvy with motor cars I knew that it was dangerous to try and unscrew the radiator cap. Third degree burns are nasty, believe me. I needed some sort of towel to insulate me so I looked in the boot. There was no towel but one of Evan's disposable nappies waved to me. Unused, I should add, and was kept for emergencies. To hell with Evan, this was my emergency!

With the radiator cap off it was plain to see that there was no water in the radiator. While contemplating my next move, I heard someone calling 'Hello! Hello!' and looked over to see an old man behind the railings of the grand house I was parked outside. '*Nam*,' (water) I replied. He nodded and raced off, coming back with a four gallon (20 litre) pail full of water.

He then insisted that he would pour it in, indicating that my clean white hospital garb was unsuitable for the job in hand. He was, of course, correct. After the

Daihatsu had swallowed 15 litres we suddenly noticed there was a veritable river coming from the left side of the engine. As fast as the radiator was filled, it emptied.

'*Mee pun hah, maak, maak*' (big problem) was the diagnosis.

As we were only one kilometre from Peter Malhotra's house (the boss of the *Pattaya Mail* newspaper group) I put the pedal to the floor and got there without the temperature gauge needle bending itself around the stop on the hot end of the scale. Peter, who is like a big brother to me (and to his staff) said he would get his garage to look at it and ran me to the hospital.

So this is why I ended up standing at the side of Sukhumvit Road waiting for one of the public buses to come along. The first two were so jam packed that the tail was dragging on the ground and the front wheels were gliding along a few inches above the tarmac. A British policeman would have swallowed his whistle at such overcrowding.

The third bus was only full, not overcrowded, so I got on, the local people all shuffled themselves around so that there was space for the *farang*, and the 20 minute trip to the hospital began. The last time I did the public transport bit, it had been 10 baht (about 17p for the UK readers) and I was very pleasantly surprised by not being ripped off with cries of 'No change,' by my driver. This time, with fuel prices rising as quickly as the Daihatsu's temperature gauge, I expected it to be more, so I offered a 20 baht note after boarding. To my amazement, a 10 baht coin was presented to me as the change. My better nature (I do have one) took control and I handed it back, saying *'Wan nee, gasoline paeng'* (gasoline is expensive today) and I was greeted by huge smiles from the driver and his wife and high *wai*'s from both of them and *'Kop khun maak!'* (Thank you very much).

The little chap who had helped me the day before had been very kind, so it was somehow fitting that I could pass some of that kindness around. You will all have heard the phrase 'What goes around, comes around.' This is used so much in Thailand that it is almost a Buddhist mantra referring to one's karma, but for me, it looks like being more related to my 'carma'.

Now if you believe in Jung's Theory of Synchronicity (I don't but it's fun to contemplate), yesterday my wife called into the local Ford dealer to enquire about the prices, as I had mentioned that I liked the look of the new Ford Focus. It turned out they had a special deal for doctors. Zero percent deposit and one percent interest on the capital sum. Suddenly, after 40 odd years of being a medico, the real reason for the hard yakka was staring me in the face. Zero percent deposit for doctors. I like the sound of this promotion. I will go to the Ford dealers this afternoon and see if I like the car. A 10 baht donation to the bus driver might just turn into a new vehicle for me. Good 'carma', I think.

Marrying the family

My mother-in-law came to stay for a few days when I started to write this chapter in my topsy-turvy life. She is a nice up-country lady from Isaan, living in a village called Sirindhorn, which is about as far East as you can go in Thailand, without actually tripping over into Laos and Cambodia. In fact if you look at the history of the place, it was once part of Laos, so it is not surprising that the people in Sirindhorn speak Lao as the first language, which is also known as 'Isaan'.

My wife picked up her mother from the bus after the 12 hour trip down to Pattaya, and proudly brought her home for her mother's first visit to our new house. In fact, this was her first visit to Pattaya in five years. The last one was to come look over this strange *farang* that her daughter wanted to marry, and apparently gave him the nod.

As she alighted from the car, I *wai*'d as one should to an elder relative such as a mother-in-law. In this case, however, she is 10 years younger than me. Thailand certainly does throw the usual stereotypes out the window. She had another girl with her, a small nugget-brown girl, dressed in a pink party dress.

'Who is this one?' I asked my wife.

'She is the daughter of my brother, the one who went away.'

'Ah, I see. How old is she?'

'She is five years old and Mum has been raising her like a daughter.'

Now, at least, I knew the connection, but I could not help looking at this little moppet. She was only about one inch taller than my two-year-old son Evan and very much smaller than three-and-a-half-year-old Miss Marisa. Having met my wife's brother once, I knew he was no giant, but this child was too small, despite not being heiress to some 'tall' genes. Nutrition for partially abandoned babies in the villages of Isaan is not the same as for the pampered bubs in the West.

I warmed to the little girl over the next few weeks and even suggested to Som that we could keep her with us and send her to school with our two children. After all, when you marry a Thai lady, you marry the family, if you didn't know already that by this stage. I have to say I was amazed when Som said, 'No, the little girl will stay with Mum, because that is the only child she has at home.'

Further questioning brought to light that my mother-in-law was probably the most maternal woman I had ever met. She had five children of her own—Som's elder sister (who died), Som and her younger brother to their Thai-Chinese father (who died when Som was nine years old), and following remarrying had another daughter and the final child, another son.

For us Westerners, that would be enough, but it was not for a resolute lady from Isaan, and is also too simplistic for an Isaan family. I have mentioned before that a young girl called Toon, whom Som refers to as her 'cousin', though sometimes she calls her a 'sister'. On the surface it is confusing. It turns out that Toon's grandmother was a younger sister of Som's grandmother, so there is a blood line there, but Toon's mother died in childbirth. Baby Toon was raised by Som's mother who also took in Toon's elder sister, who was also motherless. (The father remarried and didn't want the girls.) That makes seven, and now with the new five year old, that makes eight.

What must also be taken into account is the fact that Som did not come from a rich, land-owning family. This shows what can be achieved by Thai country families, and also explains the mystifying relationships in those families. How many times have you been introduced to 'a sister', knowing that your wife or girlfriend doesn't have a 'sister'? Now you know what the term means. It is a person from their village, probably with some genetic code sharing, but it could even be just a person raised in their family with them. All initially confusing to our rigid western minds, but like so many things in Thailand, it is best not to enquire too deeply, and just go with the flow.

Part of going with the flow does mean that our house has become the Pattaya outpost of the village in Sirindhorn. We have a spare room, and occasionally Toon, or Som's youngest brother named Kot, will stay for a night or two. In no way do they take over, but are very respectful of their *farang* brother-in-law, and they both obviously love Marisa and Evan. They, in turn enjoy the attention and will bunk in with their country relatives, as I expect would happen in the village itself, and I will find them all snuggled up together in the morning.

It sometimes takes a little time to get used to the extended family, but the children grow up experiencing that family love is a good aspect of life in Thailand.

When you arrived in Thailand, do you remember what immigration gate you came in after you got off the plane? It was called the 'Aliens' gate, you, me and ET. We are from a different planet at times.

Thrills and spills

I have to say I have probably had more sheer excitement in my life than the average doctor. Amongst the most exciting events of my life are driving an F1 car (actually a F 5000 Lola T 430, the Aussie F1 car of the day) plus many other categories of race cars, even designing and building my own car. I've also experienced the exhilaration of parachute jumping out of a perfectly good aeroplane (though it did crash one week after my jump), competing in Moto-X (starting at age 32 for three years), driving a six litre Sprint car at the speedway (when I was 40 years old), riding a speedway dirt track motorcycle (when I was 42 years old). I've also fallen through a factory roof (once was enough), went Scuba diving in the Solomon Islands, flown in everything from gliders, microlights, light planes, sea-planes, helicopters and commercial jumbo jets including sitting in the engineer's seat for the landing into the old Kai Tak airport in Hong Kong. (Amazing. It seems that you flew down the main street where you were so low you could look into the office buildings, and then turned left at the traffic lights.)

I think there's more, but nothing, repeat nothing, beats a very memorable motorcycle trip in Bangkok.

It was about 1985 and I was on holiday in the nation's capital. The congestion was worse, if anything, than it is now, as the overhead road system was still being built. My problem was that I had a most important meeting to attend, and the traffic was grid-locked, stopped, stuck and going nowhere. I was not near a *klong* (canal) to be able to take a river taxi. There was only one alternative left—a taxi motorcycle.

Working on the principle that he would be able to weave in and out of the lanes of grid-locked cars, I hailed one. This is not a difficult task. You raise your right arm and it will be immediately responded to from the nearest street corner where the motorcycle taxis congregate. My smiling rider arrived with the standard query, 'Where you go?'

'Regent Hotel, and I am in a big hurry. Must be there in 20 minutes.'

The smile broadened and I was told to throw my leg over and we were away. I was holding a large package with one hand so I put my other hand on the grip behind the seat. We had no helmets, as this was long before the legislation making helmets compulsory for motorcycle riders (although ex-prime minister Thaksin Shinawatra was shown on the front page of a national daily in 2005, riding with his entire cabinet behind him and all helmetless. I doubt they were prosecuted.)

The next 20 minutes were a mixture of terror, excitement, incredulity and awe at my rider's skills. I am not exaggerating when I say we did not stop once on the entire trip. His favourite riding area was not on the road with the congested cars, but either on the pavement, or even more amazingly on the centre median strip. These strips have a metal fence in the middle and we would ride along brushing the fence. My rider when he did this the first time did reach backwards and pull my right knee in, but I was still brushing the railings as we rode at breakneck speed. The second and third time he mounted the median strip, he did not pull my knee in, as by that stage I was supposed to have learned enough to be able to do it myself.

The prime difficulty here was stopping the natural tendency to want to lean away from the dividing fence, as this just unbalances the motorcycle, which would have seen us arrive sideways into the lanes of traffic.

At traffic lights we would leap off the median strip and ride across the front of the cars and then mount the pavement on the other side where we rode through the pedestrians, weaving from side to side and somehow missing them all.

At the next set of lights it was a jump off the pavement and across the road and onto the median strip again, with my right knee going 'zap-zap-zap-zap' once more on the railings. I had long since given up the nonchalant one handed grip on the rear grab bar, but was by then clutching onto the rider (Bangkok's answer to Moto GP champion Valentino Rossi) like an oversized koala bear hanging onto its mother. (By the way, please do not write in and tell me that koalas are not 'bears' but are actually marsupials. I know this already, but 'koala bear' sounds much better than 'Australian indigenous grey furry marsupial that lives in trees and eats eucalyptus leaves.' Interestingly, it is one of the few animals that does not drink water, but exists totally on eucalyptus leaves. So how about that for a learning exercise.)

But back to the cross-Bangkok journey. We did make it to the hotel on time. I made it to the toilet off the foyer in time without embarrassing myself in public. The bruises on my right knee settled after a few days, and I made a solemn pact to never tell a motorcycle taxi rider that I was in a hurry to go anywhere, ever again.

I have used motorcycle taxis since then, but my instructions after the destination is understood are always '*Cha Cha*' (slowly). There is just so much excitement one can take at one time. I've had all I need.

The village birthday party

When Marisa turned four we threw a birthday party for her. Well, in actual fact, it was a birthday party for the children from our village. At four years of age, children do not really understand birthdays—'That was when you came out of Mummy's tummy, and that was four years ago.' The reply 'How did I get in there?' really was opening up a can of worms which at that stage was best left unopened, so it was easier to just say we would have a party for her.

There was another reason to have a party and that was decidedly magic. Many years ago I met a Dutch magician called Henk Romeijn and his wife Maritska. You have to understand that Pattaya is a pretty small place and it is not difficult to end up in the public eye, especially if you do some presenting work on TV, as I do. Elsewhere in this book I mention the 'big fish in a small pond'' syndrome, and this is a classic case. Mata Hari restaurateur Louis Noll (Dutch Indonesian) asked if I could give Henk Romeijn some publicity, and so the connection was made. Ex-pats living in Thailand all eventually know (of) each other and that common ex-pat bond surpasses nationalities.

I am a sucker for magic shows and Henk puts on a good one, all the way from table magic in front of your eyes to large stage extravaganzas, so when Marisa's birthday was looming, and Henk and Maritska were in town at that time, I asked if they could make this birthday something special. They agreed immediately. What goes around then comes around, as the old saying goes.

I have to admit that Som was a little doubtful and thought that Marissa might have been a little too young to enjoy the show. I wasn't, however, and there were lots of other children in the village old enough to appreciate the magic. So the birthday party planning began to take form, and Som, ever the practical one, worked out that there were 14 children in our little village. We would need tables and chairs for the children and the Mums and Dads, enough of which we did not have. I put on my best 'I dunno what to do' look, and that is when Som the organiser took charge.

Thai village life has the local temple (*wat*) as its central point, and Som took me down there to hire all the necessary items for a village party. Since I was under the misguided opinion that all the temple did was hold religious ceremonies, I was about to be educated. The temple had everything. For us, tables and chairs were all we needed, and they had plenty. I asked the monk who helped us load up, how much it was to hire the items, and received that almost universal Thai reply, 'Up to you.' However, he did add that if we had no money, that was OK too, and the use of the tables and chairs was free. I thanked him profusely and we made a generous donation to the temple's electricity box.

Our car was not large enough to carry all the items, so Som asked Peter, the Swiss chap in the house opposite ours, if he could help with his pick-up truck. He immediately drove down to the temple and picked up everything we had been unable to transport ourselves. Peter has two boys, Tommy and Steven (about 8 and 10 years old), so they were automatically invited to the magic show.

And so the day of the magic show arrived and so too did the kids from the village. Danny, a Belgian chap from the hospital came too, with his little adopted Thai children, and so the multinational event grew. Almost all the children from the village have foreign Dads and Thai Mums, so it was also a multilingual event, though for the children, Thai was the common language for communication. For the adults it was English (thank goodness).

The children arranged their chairs in rows in the car-port area, while the adults arranged their tables with beers in the garden area, and the magic show with Henk Romeijn began. Marisa was draped in a magic cape and a Merlin's hat, and with an electric rabbit as his partner, Henk held the children spellbound. He also held the adults mesmerised, who by then had gravitated to the back row of the children's seats. It really was an 'event'.

For those readers from overseas who might point out that this type of birthday party can be done anywhere, sure, it can be. But how many of you (of any religion or none) can hire everything from your local church (and free if you want) find a professional magician willing to come to your house, and find neighbours who will fetch and carry (and take the equipment back again)? In today's western world this wouldn't happen. Neighbours are viewed upon with suspicion, children would not be allowed to attend a party at someone's house up the street, and costs would be prohibitive. You would probably also have to take out public liability insurance and get a certificate of lack of contagion from the Health and Safety wallahs.

Thailand is still a place where being part of a 'village' means there is a common bond, and 'trust' is not misplaced. When we go out and need to leave the children, Peter's maid Om will look after them. Or Oh, the lady one house further down, or even Marisa's boyfriend Insi's parents. Do you remember those days from your childhood? Before materialism and envy befell us. Those days can still be appreciated in Thailand, and is yet another reason why I live 'here', and not 'there'.

Dining out

In addition to some of my other columns in the *Pattaya Mail*, I also write the 'Dining Out' column. This I do under the pseudonym of 'Miss Terry Diner'—just say it quickly and you get 'mystery diner' which explains it all. However, this is a small place and Miss Terry only shields me from the newbies. I also do not wear a dress, just in case you were wondering.

Miss Terry and Madame eat out every week, to fill my 700 word column, and our respective stomachs. It's not a bad sort of a gig. Mind you, it is not quite as easy as you might imagine. There's always a downside, isn't there? The first thing you have to do is find a restaurant that wishes to be reviewed. Despite what people imagine, we do not sneak in, with cameras in false heels, while wearing a raincoat and a fake moustache. This is a very small place, we are known and I have no desire to die of lead poisoning administered by a Colt 38. Reviews are done in the open.

Secondly, our idea of a review and the restaurateur's can be totally different. We have gone to a restaurant where the food has been brought out with great pomp and circumstance, and we were told to please take the photographs. After that, the food disappeared and we were left sitting at a vacant table. From the restaurant's point of view, the review was over. From our point of view it had hardly started. And how do you get out of that one without either party losing face? With difficulty!

Remember too, that when reviewing a restaurant, the Dining Out team has to take into account the style (and prices) of the restaurant. One should not expect pre-warmed plates at a roadside eatery, but should definitely expect one in a fine dining venue.

With just 50 restaurants reviewed each year, this is but a small proportion of the restaurants in Pattaya. Ten years ago there were about 300 restaurants in Pattaya. Now there are more than 1,000 and we reviewed more than 10 significant new restaurants in 2008 alone. The culinary scene is also constantly changing. Some restaurants close before they get to their 'Grand Opening'. That's a fact.

Like most private enterprises both in Thailand and in the West, the good will survive and the not-so-good will go under. The length of time before the final submersion may be months, but it does not go past two years. Live through two low seasons and you can continue, but it will be difficult.

Pattaya is a city that exists on tourism. If, for any reason, the tourist numbers decrease, so does the size of the marketplace. And there are any number of reasons to make the tourist population dwindle. One of these is Thailand's political instability (we have currently had three governments in the span of two years), there has been unrest in the south of Thailand (for example, prospective tourists have no idea where Pattani is—it could be a suburb of Bangkok for all they know). Another reason for a decline could be the sub-prime world being in financial doldrums or the escalating cost of airfares. The restaurateurs have to compete with each other against this background, and it isn't easy. Just ask any of them.

For the sake of this item, I am going to ignore the scores of cheap 'foreign' restaurants that bob up here. In those situations, a likely lad from the UK falls in love with Thailand, Thai culture, or more usually, a go-go girl from Isaan. He feels that all he has to do is to teach his lovely bride how to cook sausages and chips and their (his) future is assured in this, his newly adopted country. Of course he has had no training in the industry but he knows that to get the punters in the door, he must undercut the established places. This he does, and trades at a loss until the savings run out and the girl of his dreams goes back to the bar, because it was more fun than being spattered with chip fat.

In the real restaurant stakes in Thailand, there are many good players. At the back of this book I have listed some that I particularly like. They are not in any particular order but do represent some of the Dining Out team's preferences in Pattaya. Thailand is a rich and varied country, and I'm delighted to say that this is also reflected in the choice and availability of restaurants. In the restaurants I have listed, I can assure you that you will enjoy the food and the ambience, there is more to enjoying dinner than munching on a well done steak.

In search of nationality

I viewed a very interesting TV documentary the other night. It was shot in the UK and involved six people who considered themselves 'very' English. These were people who would fly the cross of St. George and not the Union Jack. These people viewed themselves as 'English', and not 'British'.

In the documentary they arranged to take blood samples from these English people for DNA testing and compared their DNA against global DNA records, to see just how English they really were. The volunteers included the daughter of the Iron Maiden, Maggie Thatcher, and another very forthright lady who was an English lawyer.

In the case of Margaret Thatcher's daughter she was nothing but English. She was a true thoroughbred, and someone who could rightly bear the cross of St. George.

For the other 'truly English' people who were tested, it was nothing but bad news. There were undeniable signs of cross-border dalliances by their ancestors. This included evidence of heritage from Romany gypsies, Mongolians (Genghis Khan visits Manchester?), Iranians and other Levantine nationalities. Even Central African influences were apparent but I don't think we should blame Idi Amin, the self-proclaimed last king of Scotland, for this. The results were so shocking, that the English lawyer attempted to sue the program, claiming the results were wrong, which shows just how far some people will go to protect 'their' nationality.

So what has all that got to do with Thailand? When I first began dating my wife to be, I noticed that her face was somewhat different to the usual Thai faces. Her skin was also lighter than most, which was not from overdosing on whitening creams, incidentally the most heavily advertised product on Thai TV.

'Are you really Thai?' I asked her one day.

'Yes, *roi* percent,' (100 percent) was her proud reply.

At first I accepted this as you try, if possible, to keep the first date questioning to a minimum. However, later in our relationship I was to find that her maternal grandmother was a Laotian who married a Thai soldier stationed at the Thai/Laos border, making her mother Lao-Thai. Her paternal grandparents were unknown, but she did know that her long-deceased father was Thai-Chinese. Forgetting Mendel's theories and all the XX and XY chromosomes, this information simply means that my wife is Lao-Thai-Chinese. This was somewhat contrary to the 100 percent Thai identity she had claimed previously.

So, what really constitutes a Thai nationality? To answer this, you need to study linguistics and have a passable understanding of the different kingdoms and races (and battles) in Southeast Asia. Let's talk about linguistics first. The study of different languages has identified a group of people who speak 'Tai' (not to be confused with 'Thai' which was the name adopted for Thailand after Siam became a constitutional monarchy). Are you still with me? Good. You're not confused yet? Even better.

It would appear, according to the linguistic historians, that the Tai speakers migrated from Southern China, and came down further south into the plains of the Chaopraya River, which would eventually bring this group to Ayutthya, once the capital of Siam. In fact there is an area in South China where something that sounds like Thai is still spoken, but it is actually Tai. So, are the Thai just Chinese? The answer to that is both yes and no. Undoubtedly the majority of Thai people today would have some kind of Chinese genetic code, but like all things in Thailand, it is never quite that simple.

You have to also delve into some history. The Sri Lankans and the Indians from the west moved across what is now Burma and Southern China and funnelled down into central Siam, bringing with them the Buddhist religion, and enough suit material to be able to open a tailor shop on every street corner.

Also from the west came the Burmese, generally in the form of raiding parties or armies, occupying many areas of what is now Thailand for decades. The animosity is still evident today, and the Thais have not forgiven the Burmese for their sacking of the Siamese capital Ayutthya in 1767. Burmese seed was also spilled on the way, so there are some Burmese genetic codes floating around today's Thailand. For that matter the Burmese are another polyglot nation of tribes who only came together to rid the area of the British.

To the east lay the countries of the Mon and Khmer, all of whom at some stages ruled parts of modern day Thailand, and some of whom were influenced by Brahman India. Their peoples intermixed and intermarried with the Tai speaking inhabitants to make it even more difficult for the geneticists several hundreds of years later.

Let's look at Laos in the late 1800's. The Isaan area encompassed what is now Northeast Thailand and Laos, and was all Lao speaking, but was really a vassal state of Siam, paying their dues to the Siamese kings. In 1893, King Chulalongkorn was being threatened by the French, who even sent warships up the Chaopraya. To avoid a senseless all-out war, the area to the east of the Mekong River was ceded to the French to become French Indo-China, whilst the Isaan (Lao speaking) area to the west of the Mekong became Siamese, ruled from Bangkok by legislation in 1899. It was no longer a self-governing vassal state and Thai soldiers were sent to guard the Thai-Lao border. This included my wife's maternal grandfather.

That was not much over 100 years ago, so it is relatively easy to see how my '100 percent Thai' wife had a Thai soldier grandfather, a Lao grandmother, and a Thai-Chinese father. This is shown by the fact that my wife speaks 'Isaan' (Lao) with her mother and her siblings, but speaks Thai with officials and English with me.

So what about our children? My father was English (geographically even if not genetically and it is too late to prove or disprove as I have no desire to have him exhumed, and since he was cremated, that puts an end to that line of enquiry). My mother is fiercely Scottish from the Highlands, so that makes me 'British' even though I was born in Ireland. Therefore young Mr. Evan and Little Miss Marisa are Thai-Laos-Chinese-British. It was also very interesting for me to see that both the children carry the Mongolian Blue Spot, the skin pigment sign on the buttocks denoting direct descent from the Chinese Mongol hordes of Genghis Khan, which may go some way towards explaining Evan's violent temper tantrums. It's either that or the fact he is in the middle of the terrible twos.

Now, apart from all this discourse on nationalities being of great academic interest, I have to say I also find it all a little sad. How many millions of people have died for 'their country', lands to which they may have only possessed a very minimal birthright? In WW III, who will Evan fight for—Thailand, Laos, China or the

UK? I shall tell him to side with the Chinese, I think. There are more of them than anyone else.

The big fish in a small pond syndrome

I never had any burning desire to be an author. However, like many people, I always thought that there was a book in my head, a collection of some of the many and varied experiences I had lived through over the years. I even had the title. It was to be called 'Biscuits in Bed' —or 'The crumbs I had slept with!' Of course, that was all said with a tongue in the cheek and a big smile.

When 'Farang, Thailand through the eyes of an expat', my first book was released, I have to admit I was very nervous. The release was to be held at Jameson's Irish Pub and the landlord Kim Fletcher had hung a large poster announcing the book launch. The scheduled time for the launch was 7 p.m. and I got there at 6.30 p.m. to see the Bookazine staff already there and several copies of the book on display. I felt very proud for a couple of milliseconds, before the fear took over.

I admitted to Kim that this was like throwing a party, and I was unsure if anyone was going to come. After all, this was my first and only book. I began to feel a tremble coming on, but Kim, a past master at this kind of thing, prescribed me a large glass of white wine. The second one drowned the butterflies in my stomach and 7 p.m. arrived.

I couldn't believe what I was seeing, when a whole host of people came in the door and actually bought the book. I was given a seat in the corner and for the next hour and a half I just sat there signing copies. Not only was I published, but I was now an author whose books had been purchased. Another wine later and I was smiling like the proverbial Cheshire cat, displaying my dental records to the world, or to Pattaya at least.

Many people do not know that I have always had a dreadful head for names. People I know very well were buying the book and standing in line for a dedication and my autograph, their names, however, continued to escape me.

Suddenly I thought of how to get round the amnesia. 'How exactly do you spell your name?' I would ask, adding, 'Some people have different ways of spelling their name, like J-o-h-n or J-o-n.'

The ruse worked perfectly, and I was saved from eternal embarrassment. 'Yes, that's D-a-v-i-d, and there you are. Thank you for buying it.'

In fact, the initial sales were so good that Bookazine continued to run out of stock, and people began clamouring for a copy. I was asked to address many groups in Pattaya to talk about what it was like to be an 'author' and how I managed to get to that exalted state.

For those who have not heard how this occurred, here is the true and unexpurgated story on how I became an author. It began 40 years ago, when I was working in Gibraltar, that strange rock hanging off the bottom of Spain. When I was there, Spain had blockaded Gibraltar, so we were basically under siege. A very interesting time, but that tale is for another book, another day.

My first wife had received magazines from Australia and one of these was the Australian *Women's Weekly*. Women's magazines in Australia have totally incongruous names. The popular *Women's Weekly* comes out monthly, and the second most popular, the *Woman's Day* comes out weekly. What makes the situation even more incongruous is that both are owned by the same publishing house, Australian Consolidated Press. I think it all comes from standing on your head all day, down-under.

Women's Weekly was running a travel competition and offering money for interesting travel stories. Our current state of being under siege in Gibraltar was sure to be of interest, so I suggested to my wife that she should write in. However, she had no desire to put paper in the typewriter, so I said I would do it myself and wrote in. Damn me, if I didn't get a great fat cheque in return. At that moment I decided to become a writer. It paid better than the salary I was receiving being a Junior House Officer on British National Health

Scheme wages. Though, to be honest, that was not too difficult in those days.

It was then that my parallel careers of medicine and writing began. I found I could write about my passion for racing cars as there were plenty of motoring magazines willing to pay for articles. I also found that there was a ready market for travel stories as well—and if one was just a little bit canny, there were free trips to be had. One of these free trips was to Fiji. They had just had a coup, so I rang their national tourism office and told them that nobody would be willing to come on holidays from Australia because they were too afraid of the country's political instability. I also informed them that I was prepared to come over and write about the real situation; at their expense.

I did not have to wait long for their decision. The next day I received a call from the Fiji Tourism Board who said they would arrange flights over and back for my wife and I, and accommodation at seven different resorts for seven nights and a car would be placed at my disposal. Naturally, this was all *gratis*.

Pity the poor travel writer, what an arduous life! In actual fact you do work hard as a travel writer. Arriving at any location means a lot handshaking and note taking before you are shown to your room. You cannot just throw your bag on the bed. The first thing you have to do is photograph the accommodation interior, the view from the window and the loo. Only after that can you sit down and work out what you are going to do at that particular locale before attacking the room fridge.

By the time I arrived in Thailand in 1997, just in time for the Asian economic crash, I was a seasoned writer. I had written for many magazines, as well as having a weekly column in one of Rupert Murdoch's daily newspapers and had several overseas trips under my belt. With this background it was relatively easy to convince Peter Malhotra, the MD of the *Pattaya Mail*, that I should start writing for him.

My writing career flourished, but whilst I had written thousands of articles, I had not yet written a book. I had some stories I had filed away, just in case I did write that book one day, but that was as far as it went. I had heard all the horror stories of other prospective authors who had sent their slaved-over manuscripts off to various publishers, only to get a reject slip. It was said, by those who purported to know, that after you can paper a wall with reject slips, you might just get lucky. I was totally put off. My ego could not cope with rejection of that magnitude.

This, I feel, is where serendipity came in. I had just read a book that had been published by Maverick House, and since I have always been somewhat of a maverick, I decided to write to them and see if they were interested in a book about an ex-pats viewpoint on life in Thailand. They were, and asked me to send some chapters. With my heart in my mouth, I did, and received an email back with a contract attached. I was so taken aback I was still giggling when I rang my wife to tell her the good news. I signed the contract, sent over my 30 short stories and sat back. After a couple of months, the editor who had been assigned to my book emailed to say they were very happy with the book, but it was only 30,000 words long. The book contract I had signed said they needed 60,000 words, they asked could I send over the rest by the end of May 2007. This was the end of March.

This was decision time. I could either pull out and admit defeat, or I could keep my nose down and my bum up for the next two months. I could not let the chance of a getting my book published just disappear. It involved furious writing for eight weeks, but we did it. I say 'we' because my wife had to put up with me banging away on the keyboard every evening and every weekend. There were sacrifices all round, heaven help any child who interrupted me wanting a glass of water.

The book was released at the end of August 2007 in the UK and the following month in Thailand. It is difficult to describe the feeling of holding one's first book in one's hand. There really is a feeling of having accomplished something in life. I held it in my hand for a full five minutes before I could even open it. My second action was to send a copy off to my dear old mother, who really had made it all possible. She mentioned the fact that my late father would have been so proud.

'He'd have been dancing down the street with it,' she said. He probably would have. Dad was an extrovert. Perhaps that's where I got it from.

As the book took off, I was asked to do some interviews for TV and magazines and to speak at various service clubs and organisations. As an author, I had become a 'celebrity' in the ex-pat community in Thailand. This was not why I wrote the book, but does show the fact that you can become a big fish in Thailand, as long as you choose a small enough pond.

I am very pleased that everyone seems to have enjoyed my first book, so I can only hope that they enjoy this one as much.

Dining out & recipes

Here is my personal list of recommended restaurants in Pattaya. The order is not really significant, but the category the restaurants are in is probably more important. I have also made comments after each listing, which will also act as a guide. This is not an advertisement for any restaurant, as nobody mentioned here has paid to be included in the list. Rather, I am simply sharing what I consider to be the best places, through my own personal dining experiences. Should any of the restaurants listed here offer me a bottle of wine the next time I go in, however, I think I won't decline!

Straight into the top level:

- Casa Pascal—superb anytime and Sunday Brunch is most enjoyable.
- Grill Room and Wine Cellar—the Royal Cliff Beach Resort at its best.

- Mata Hari—with wine bar and restaurant, the best of both worlds.
- Mantra—spectacular dining with multiple cuisines.
- Bruno's—predictably top class.
- Manhattans—the steak specialist in Nirvana Place.
- Minus 5 degrees supper club and Ice Bar —amazing decor.

Intermediate Level:
- Poseidon—with Kim and Pascal Schnyder at the helm, now rising to its potential.
- Amor—Around forever, and forever first class.
- Café des Amis—wonderful French colonial ambience.

Great Solid Meals:
- Jameson's Irish Pub—pub grub, enormous portions and not expensive.
- Hard Rock Café—eat to the beat, where else on Beach Road?
- Greg's Kitchen—lashings of British food and inexpensive.
- Café New Orleans—sanity in Soi Pattayaland 2, with different cuisine.
- King Seafood—another long-stay restaurant Walking Street over the water.

- Great American Rib—for great American ribs.
- Captain's Corner—around for years and still great value.
- Jomtien Boathouse—you'll never leave hungry.

'Ethnic' Restaurants:
- Don Joe—Italian like Mamma used to make, great venue on Walking Street.
- The Taj—Indian food, good venue 3rd Road.
- Yamato—Japanese, the new venue (behind Carrefour) has given Yamato a new lease of life.
- Au Bon Coin—unofficial French embassy, wonderful French cuisine.
- Trattoria Toscana—new venue on Beach Road, and decidedly Italian.
- Tikka 2—crazily cheap Indian food in Jomtien Complex.

Some 'newbies' worth visiting:
- La Luna—top end 3rd Road, also European and faultless.
- Seafood Emporium—opposite Jomtien Market, marinated seafood concept.
- Pizza Pizza—in The Avenue, Italian with a flourish!

- Romanasia—best bargain in Pattaya, marvel at the décor!
- News Café—European food in Chateau Dale Jomtien.
- Grappa—Italian, in the Woodlands Suites, huge pizzas.

There are many more restaurants on offer that I have mentioned and regular visitors to Pattaya will have their own favourites. In the list above, we haven't even started to look at the plethora of good restaurants in Bangkok.

So here's a few we have tried in Bangkok:
- Le Normandie (French)—in the Oriental Hotel. Take your gold card!
- D'Sens (French)—in the Dusit Thani. Hit the gold card again.
- Rang Mahal (Indian)—top floor Rembrandt Hotel.
- Zanotti (Italian)—make sure the gold card is topped up.

And if you are taking in Chiang Mai, try these:
- Le Coq d'Or (French)—set in the old British consulate.
- Fujian (Chinese)—in the Mandarin Oriental Dhara Dhevi.
- The House (Pacific Rim Fusion)—for culinary surprises.

So there you are; some starting points for a culinary tour of Thailand. Food-wise, this is an amazing country, and don't forget the thousands of Thai food restaurants either.

To finish this small section on food, I am giving you recipes for a some Thai dishes. This first one is the world famous Tom Yum Goong. It is a simple recipe to make in the traditional manner. The Thai recipe calls for the heads to be left on the prawns, but if cooking for predominantly non-Thai friends, remove the heads (and the shell) before cooking. This recipe also shows you when to intervene in checking the seasoning. The final taste should be spicy-sour and a little salty.

Tom Yum Goong

Serves 4

Ingredients

Prawns, shelled	12 medium
Chicken stock	600 ml
Mushrooms, halved	150 gm
Kaffir lime leaves	3
Lemongrass chopped	3 stalks
Chilies, small green	4
Coriander leaf	1/4 cup
Lime juice	3 tbspns
Fish sauce	1/2 tbspn

Cooking Method

In a saucepan boil the chicken stock, and then add the lemongrass, lime leaves and mushrooms. Add the prawns and cook for around 5 minutes. Remove from the heat and add the chillies, coriander, lime juice and fish sauce and allow to stand for five minutes. Now check the seasoning, adding more lime juice or fish sauce, or breaking up the green chilies if more spiciness is required. If required, place over the heat for one minute before serving with steamed rice to eat this in Thai style.

Sopa's Tom Kha Gai
Serves 4

Ingredients

Sliced chicken breast fillet	500 gm
Lobo Tom Kha paste	1 packet
(available in supermarkets)	
Coconut milk, canned	600 ml
Lemongrass cut into 1 cm pieces	1 small stick
Lemon or lime juice	10 ml
Chilli (chopped, no seeds)	2 medium
Fish sauce (Tiparos is good)	50 ml
Sugar	3 tspns
Kaffir lime leaves	1
Water	1 cup
Straw mushrooms (whole, canned)	50 gm
Coriander (fresh, shredded)	1 tbspn

Cooking Method

Put the coconut milk and Tom Kha paste into a pot and bring to the boil. Add chicken breast pieces and bring to the boil again over a medium heat.

Add the rest of the ingredients, other than the coriander, and boil for another two minutes over a medium heat.

This can be served immediately, if in a hurry, or allowed to simmer for a while to enhance the spiciness.

Sprinkle the coriander over the soup just before serving.